MW01489990

OUTDOOR GAS GRIDDLE

Cookbook

*Let Your Taste Buds Go Crazy with Countless Mouthwatering, Easy Recipes and 31 Secret Cooking Hacks to Effortlessly Become the **#1 Chef** of the Neighborhood*

Richard Henry Campbell

© Copyright 2022 by Richard Henry Campbell - All rights reserved.

The content contained within this book may not be reproduced, duplicated or transmitted without direct written permission from the author or the publisher.

Under no circumstances will any blame or legal responsibility be held against the publisher, or author, for any damages, reparation, or monetary loss due to the information contained within this book, either directly or indirectly.

Legal Notice:

This book is copyright protected. It is only for personal use. You cannot amend, distribute, sell, use, quote or paraphrase any part, or the content within this book, without the consent of the author or publisher.

Disclaimer Notice:

Please note the information contained within this document is for educational and entertainment purposes only. All effort has been executed to present accurate, up to date, reliable, complete information. No warranties of any kind are declared or implied. Readers acknowledge that the author is not engaged in the rendering of legal, financial, medical or professional advice. The content within this book has been derived from various sources. Please consult a licensed professional before attempting any techniques outlined in this book.

By reading this document, the reader agrees that under no circumstances is the author responsible for any losses, direct or indirect, that are incurred as a result of the use of the information contained within this document, including, but not limited to, errors, omissions, or inaccuracies.

"Barbecue may not be the road to world peace, but it's a start."

Anthony Bourdain

Table of Contents

Introduction

The Outdoor Gas Griddle Cookbook contains so many mouth-watering recipes that are perfect for any occasion, or just when you want to cook up something tasty for your family and friends. Each recipe is completely described in great detail so you can easily follow the instructions.

The best thing about these recipes is that they are cooked on a flat-top griddle. The flat-top griddle is one of the most popular appliances used by chefs and home cooks alike.

All the recipes make great-tasting dishes perfect for any celebration. With these recipes, you will be able to cook delicious meals in no time at all. This unique kind of griddle can be used to make a variety of foods, including bread, breakfast items, desserts, and much more.

This cookbook will not only show you the best ways and techniques to grill, but it will also provide you with a bunch of beneficial tips and a large array of sumptuous griddled recipes that you can only find in this cookbook. And if you think it is impossible to come up with your own favorite recipes using different types of meat, like chicken parmesan, crunchy chicken fingers, chicken nuggets, fish and chips, zesty cuts of meat, and different types of veggies, meat, chicken and fish, then you should think again, because it is now completely possible with the help of this cookbook. I will also talk in this cookbook about the best cooking techniques to control the temperature; with the help of a griddle, maintain your grill flat, and don't give up on a large array of sumptuous recipes you will never regret tasting. This is the perfect grill book for you if you want to show off a large array of sumptuous griddled dishes. You will see in here just how easy it is not only to get a perfectly cooked meal but also to get a lot of attention when you serve good food. But with this grill book, I want you to know that all kinds of meat are included.

Gas griddles are known to be amongst the most useful and easy-to-use cooking tools you can use outdoors. The best part is that gas griddles are very affordable, but it can be very challenging to choose the best gas griddle for the money.

Maintenance of a griddle is an important thing if you want to have it last for a long period. If you don't take enough care of your electric flat top griddle, it will not last as long as it should. You must always clean your griddle with warm water and soap after use.

Outdoor griddles have long been used as cookware and are widely used in restaurants and diners to offer us mesmerizing hot staples and dishes.

The Outdoor Gas Griddle

What Does it Do?

A griddle is a cooking surface on which you can prepare all kinds of food, like pancakes, bacon, eggs, or sausage. Unlike a stovetop or the oven, you can use it to cook a large variety of things at once. Your flat top griddle provides up to 720 inches of professional-grade griddle for your backyard or anywhere you go. You know how to produce professional standard meals and get the same results as professional chefs achieve every single time you cook. Your flat top griddle is made with professional-grade materials and provides professional quality heat in the form of 60,000 BTU of cooking power with four independent cooking zones. This means you can carefully control everything you cook with individual controls for each zone. Eggs don't cook properly at the same temperature as a steak, and your griddle allows you to cook both perfectly at the same time.

Because it's built from industrial-grade materials, your griddle will be a versatile appliance for many years to come. The frame of the griddle is built with super-durable powder-coated steel. The burners are made from restaurant-grade stainless steel and are guaranteed to produce perfectly even and powerful heat for years to come. Once you've spent some time with your griddle you might even consider getting rid of your more conventional gas or charcoal grills.

What Problems Does It Solve?

It takes a lot of hard work to get a great meal on the table. Cooking is even harder if you're not getting professional quality results. One of the main problems people encounter when they try to cook is uneven heat from their traditional grills. Not only does this make cooking challenging, but it also makes food taste terrible.

Who is it Good For?

Because an outdoor griddle is large enough to cook all the elements of a complete meal at the same time, it is perfect for families who love perfectly prepared backyard favorites like burgers, steaks, and veggies, but it's also perfect for families who love to make big breakfasts. Prepare eggs, bacon, hashbrowns, and pancakes for everyone at the same time.

Do you love to cook big meals on the go? An outdoor griddle is perfect for camping and tailgating because it is easy to transport and set up. Pack it up for your next camping trip and set it up when you want to make an amazing outdoor meal. An outdoor griddle is also perfect for anyone who loves making freshly griddled food for a professional tailgate party. Since your griddle easily fits in the trunk of a car, you can take it with you to the game and set it up in minutes. Impress the whole parking lot with the amazing food you make for your fellow fans.

Who is it NOT Good For?

Everyone loves food cooked in the open air, but if you don't have a large enough outdoor space in which to use the griddle, this may not be for you. A good rule of thumb is that you can use the griddle anywhere you would use a conventional gas or charcoal grill. If you have the space and don't already have a grill, you should be good to go. Also, if you plan to use the griddle in cramped quarters, it might be difficult to maneuver the flat top griddle around because it is quite large. The key to cooking both the right food on the griddle and producing professional results is using the right temperature. When most people cook on griddles, they burn their food. One of the main reasons for this is that they do not have precise control of the temperature. Because your griddle has four individual grilling zones, you can create perfect heat distribution and allow your food to cook at exactly the right temperatures to create delectable and appetizing meals.

A Few Cautions

Because outdoor griddles use an external propane tank, you will want to exercise caution while connecting and disconnecting the tank. Always make sure all connection points are clean and free of debris. When attaching the hose to the tank, make sure the valve is completely tight before allowing gas to flow to the griddle.

Your griddle's cold-rolled steel flat top produces amazing results, but because it gets very hot, you should make sure children are always supervised when near the griddle.

What Are its Health Benefits?

Griddles cover a whole host of risks. Charcoal fires increase the risk of flames in your yard. But did you know that cooking with charcoal also improves your risk of cancer? The sequence of charcoal and soaking fats causes a variety of compounds that are considered carcinogenic. And you do not just breathe in these chemicals once you grill. They're covering your food! An outdoor griddle, on the other hand, uses no charcoal and is much safer to use.

A Brief History of Grilling

You may not be surprised to hear that grilling food is a pretty old technique. It goes back over half a million years. Early humans found that meat cooked over fire was more nutritious than raw meat. The reason? Bioavailability. In short, cooking meat changes the structure of proteins and fats, allowing them to be more efficiently digested and absorbed by the body. Until the 1940s, grilling was mostly something that people did around campfires, but after World War II and the expansion of suburbs, the popularity of backyard grilling skyrocketed. By the 1950s, the backyard BBQ was a staple of family entertainment, and it remains this way today.

Better Than Conventional Grills?

Since the invention of the burger, the debate has raged over whether a grill or a flat-top griddle does the best job. While it's true that grills offer burgers a smokier flavor, does that really result in a better burger? After years of research, burger experts concluded that the flat top griddle is superior to the grill for one simple reason: it allows the burger to cook in its juices rather than have all of those juices fall through the grate and into the fire. The end result is a more evenly cooked, juicier, more flavorful burger.

Modern Gas Griddles

When most people think of griddles, they either picture a small countertop griddle that you plug in or a giant flat top that sits in the kitchen of a diner. Because the griddle is so perfect for cooking such a wide variety of foods, the invention of the modern gas griddle makes perfect sense. By marrying the idea of a propane grill with the cooking surface of a griddle, you get an appliance that is both versatile and portable.

How to Use the Outdoor Gas Griddle

The Outdoor Flat Top Griddle is one of the greatest reasonable gas griddle devices compared to other devices available in the market. It is available in two different sizes; one is 28 inches and the other is 36-inch size. The 28-inch gas griddle is made up of a stainless-steel frame and comes with a 470-square-inch cooking surface area. It is complete with two H-shaped big-size gas rings to each burner be able to make 15000 BTU, and both the burners together produce 30000 BTU heat. The 36-inch gas griddle offers a 720 square inch large size cooking area to cook food for a whole family at one time. The gas griddle is loaded with four H-shape large-size gas burners. Altogether, these burners can produce 6000 BTU of heat. Every one of the burners is equipped with an individual control switch so you can easily control them independently.

The Outdoor griddle is easy to assemble and built with high-quality stainless steel coated with black powder coating. The main cooking surface area is made up of thick rolled steel material. The griddle has a battery power ignition system started by just push-button ignition and is capable of producing a maximum of 350°F temperature. The four heavy-duty burners heat the cooking area very quickly. The Outdoor gas griddle comes with a bottom shelf, two convenient side-mounted shelves, and a propane tank holder. You can easily move the gas griddle outdoor cooking appliance with the help of four caster wheels. You can lock two wheels among these four wheels to keep your appliance steady in your backyard.

Its large 720 square inches cooking surface area is capable of handling a large quantity of food. It is capable to hold 16 steaks, 72 hot dogs, or 28 hamburgers at a time. It is also capable of cooking two different foods at the same time but with different temperature settings. When you cook eggs, it is not suitable to cook them at 60000BTU heat or the same temperature setting suitable for steak. The griddle allows you to individually control all four heating zones as per your recipe needs at the same time.

Seasoning Your Outdoor Griddle

When you buy a new griddle, it is recommended that before using the griddle, you season it with the proper seasoning method to make a non-stick layer over the cooking area and avoid scratching while cooking your food. You just need to follow the simple seasoning steps given below to improve your griddle cooking efficiency. Before starting seasoning, make sure you have collected all items and supplies needed during the seasoning process. These items and supplies include a bucket of water, tongs or heatproof gloves, soap powder, salt, a stick, and a cast-iron conditioner.

Clean your brand-new griddle with soapy water

Put 2 liters of warm water into a bucket and some soap. Mix the soap and water solution with the help of a stick. Then pour a small amount of soapy water over the griddle cooking surface and thoroughly rub it over the griddle surface with the help of a paper towel.

If you are using an old griddle then skip this soapy water step; this step may damage the coating area of the griddle.

Heat the griddle for 10 to 15 minutes

Turn on all the burners with their maximum temperature settings and allow the griddle to heat up for 10 to 15 minutes. After some time, you will notice that the top of the griddle turns brown. Then move to the next step.

Spread oil over the griddle surface

You can choose your favorite oil for seasoning the griddle. Always use high fatty acid oil like extra virgin olive oil, vegetable oil, coconut oil, flaxseed oil, or others to coat your griddle. Take 2 to 3 tablespoons of oil and spread them over the griddle surface. Use a paper towel to spread it equally all over the griddle surface. You can also use a cast iron conditioner for coating the griddle surface. Then move to the next step.

Fire the griddle again

Ignite all the burners at their max temperature position and leave it for 15 to 30 minutes at the max setting. You will notice the griddle turns black after some time, and the oil begins smoking when it reaches its smoke point. Wait until the smoke completely disappears.

Turn off griddle

Turn off the griddle after completing the first cycle and let it cool down for at least 10 minutes. After that, repeat the same procedure again and again until the griddle has turned dark brown. It requires 3 to 4 repetitions.

Final touch

Wipe the griddle with high-quality extra virgin oil or cast-iron conditioner to prevent it from oxidation. Now your griddle seasoning process is completed successfully.

Essential Tools for Griddle

Three main necessary tools are necessary for you to become a master in griddle cooking. These tools are oil bottles, spatulas, and scrapers which make outdoor griddle cooking easy. You can also use extra tools if you want to baste, steam, press, and blacken your food.

Spatula

This is one of the necessary tools used to flip, spread, mix, and lift your favorite foods like pancakes, burgers, eggs, veggies, omelets, and more. It is a kind of flat, broad, and flexible tool with an ergonomic handle made up of sturdy stainless-steel material and available in large, medium, and small sizes.

Scraper

The scraper is a sharp blade-like tool used to clean your griddle surface from debris. The scraper is a wide stainless-steel blade that comes with an ergonomic slip-resistant grip, which provides perfect control when scraping and digging over a griddle.

Squeeze Bottles

Squeeze bottles are easy tools to spread oils and water while griddling your food. The squeeze bottles are made of high-quality BPA-free plastic.

Round Basting Cover

The basting cover is made up of stainless-steel material and comes with a safety handle. A basting cover is a multipurpose tool used to steam veggies, melt cheese, and more. Use a 12-inch big-size basting cover that is capable of holding a large portion of your food and several patties at a time.

Bacon Grill Press

The grill press is made up of cast iron and comes with a wooden handle grip for safety purposes. It is ideal for flattening bacon, hamburgers, and sandwiches, and is also used as a steak weight. The main purpose of using a press grill is to remove excess grease from burgers.

Benefits of Using the Outdoor Gas Griddle

There are lots of benefits to cooking your food on an outdoor gas griddle. Let's see all these benefits one by one.

Large and Flat Cooking Surface

One of the main benefits of the outdoor gas griddle is its large and flat cooking surface. The large cooking area allows you to cook more food items at once, and flipping food is easy compared to a frying pan. You can use the griddle to cook a large quantity of food. The Outdoor griddle is capable of holding 72 hotdogs, 28 hamburgers, or 16 steaks in a single cooking batch. Due to the large cooking surface, it doesn't hold moisture and gives you a crispy cooking result. It is one of the perfect choices for bigger families who love to enjoy food like eggs, bacon, hotdogs, burgers, and veggies at the same time at backyard parties.

Excellent build quality

Outdoor gas grills are made up of high-quality stainless-steel materials. The main cooking surface is made up of rolled high-quality 7-gauge steel. The entire body surface is covered with a black powder coating which protects it from rust.

Runs on Propane gas

Outdoor gas grills use propane gas to cook your food. Compared to charcoal fuel, propane gas never creates smoke and harmful gases while cooking food in your backyard. Propane griddles are easy to start, all you need to do is turn the dial and the burner fires up. The gas griddle is capable of maintaining a steady temperature. Your griddle takes less than 15 minutes to reach its maximum temperature.

Versatile

The Outdoor gas griddle is one of the most versatile outdoor cooking appliances and enables you to cook most foods over a smooth cooking surface. The Outdoor gas griddle is equipped with 4 burners which allows you to operate them individually. The griddle is capable of cooking different types of food at different temperatures at the same time. You can cook pancakes, eggs, waffles, steaks, burgers, hot dogs, and more with perfection on a flat-top gas griddle.

Easy to clean

Cleaning the flat-top griddle is one of the easy tasks; you just need to clean the greasy cooking area. To clean grease, you can use a spatula or griddle to scrape up grease. Use a paper towel to wipe the cooking surface and finally give a touch-up with a scouring pad.

How to Store and Maintain Your Seasoned Griddle Properly

Proper storage and maintenance are necessary to increase the lifespan of your griddle. The following steps guide you in the storage and maintenance of your griddle.

After each use, clean your griddle

When you start using your griddle it seasons automatically after each use. Cleaning is one of the important steps to keep your griddle clean and hygienic. Use hot water and a paper towel to clean the griddle surface. Do not use soapy water to clean the cooking surface and use the scraper to clean the cooking area. You can clean the greasy surface with clean and dry paper towels.

Remove Rust

If you find any rust spots over the griddle then use 40 or 60 low grit sandpaper or you can also use steel wool to remove the rust spots; scrub them properly.

Coat the griddle after cleaning

After finishing the cleaning process, give a thin coat of cooking spray over the griddle cooking surface to prevent rust build up on the cooking surface area of the griddle.

Store and maintain the griddle

After finishing all the cleaning steps, store your griddle in a cool and dry place. To prevent dust, always keep your griddle under the cover and keep it away from humid areas.

Pro Tips

Season the Cooking Surface

Like most high-quality cooking appliances, the cold-rolled steel cooking surface of your Outdoor Griddle needs to be properly seasoned to ensure optimal cooking results. So, you may be asking, "what is seasoning?" Before non-stick coatings existed, there was only one way to make sure food didn't stick to the cooking surface. By creating a layer of burnt-on oil, you will not only achieve a perfect non-stick surface, but you will also protect the cooking surface from scratches and oxidation. Let's get started. First, use soap and water to thoroughly wash the cooking surface. Use a cloth to dry the surface. Next, apply a small amount of oil to the cooking surface. The best oils to use are those with a high smoke point like vegetable or canola oils. Use a paper towel to spread the oil evenly across the cooking surface. Turn on all four burners and set the temperature to 275°F. Wait until the oil begins to smoke and the surface begins to darken. Once it is smoking, turn off the burners and allow the griddle to cool. Repeat this process two to three more times until the entire surface is evenly dark. Now your griddle is naturally non-stick and protected from damage and rust.

Keep your Griddle Working from Season to Season

Because you are most likely going to keep your griddle outside, you will need to make sure to do a few things before you store it and before you use it again after being stored. Before you store it, make sure to disconnect the gas tank and store it away from the griddle with a cap on the valve. You can also purchase a cover for the griddle to keep out insects and dust. When you are ready to start using your griddle again, make sure to check the burner area for spider webs. Webs are flammable and can cause flare-ups if you do not clean them out before cooking. Check the level in your gas tank to make sure you have enough fuel to start cooking. Once the tank is attached and you are ready to cook, it's a good idea to perform a new seasoning on the cooking surface. Simply follow the instructions above, and your griddle will be good as new.

The Best Way to Clean Your Griddle

After each use, you will want to clean your griddle, but your griddle should not be cleaned like regular pots and pans. Since you want to build up a nice coating of seasoning to protect your griddle and get the best possible results, you need to make sure not to use things like dish soap to clean the cooking surface. Most detergents have a grease-cutting ingredient and this will eat right through your layer of seasoning. The best way to clean your griddle is the way the pros do in restaurants: with a griddle scraper and hot water. You can purchase a griddle scraper, which is designed to get rid of any bits of food left behind without sacrificing the seasoning layer you've achieved. To remove things like Fat: or sauces, a wash with very hot water will dissolve most things, which you can then scrape away. While you don't have to season your grill after every cleaning, continuous seasoning will ensure that your griddle stays dark and shiny.

Invest in the Proper Tools

Since the Outdoor Griddle is a professional-grade piece of equipment, you should have professional-grade cooking tools to get the most out of it. While you may have an array of spatulas in the kitchen, to get the best out of your griddle, we recommend buying two long metal spatulas. These spatulas are not only durable, but they also allow you to transport and flip a large amount of food at the same time. They are also thin and flexible, so you can scoop up things like a whole hashbrown without dropping anything. Also recommended are at least one pair of long-handled metal tongs which will allow you to reach anywhere on the griddle without worrying about getting burned.

Try Different Cooking Fats

Unlike a traditional grill which allows any cooking Fat: to fall onto the coals or gas jets, the Outdoor Griddle keeps your cooking Fat: right where you want it: on your food! Because of this, you can experiment with different flavors of cooking Fat: to optimize your results. Different oils impart different flavors, but they also work differently from each other. Olive oil imparts a robust and sometimes spicy black pepper flavor that gives an extra richness to food. However, the problem with olive oil is that it has a pretty low smoke point, which means that over a certain temperature, the oil will start to taste burned. Use olive oil for foods you are cooking at lower to medium temperature, but avoid it for foods cooked over high heat. If you're looking for oil for high-heat cooking, try canola or regular vegetable oil. They will allow you to cook to high heat without that unpleasant burnt taste. And of course, butter packs more flavor than almost anything, but it also has a tendency to burn, so use butter for low-heat cooking or for foods you plan to cook quickly.

The Ultimate Burger

For centuries, mankind has quested after the perfect burger. Since its invention, burger chefs have argued about the best way to grind it, form the patties, and, of course... the best way to cook it. Some say you have to use fancy wagyu beef imported from Japan; some say the best method is high heat over charcoal. Well, we're going to put the debate to rest once and for all. The first key to the best burger you've ever had is Fat: content. If you go to your local supermarket, you usually choose between 20% Fat: or 10% fat. For the perfect burger, this will not do. The perfect burger has between 25 and 30% fat, and the best way to achieve this is to grind it yourself using a combination of chuck and short rib. If you don't feel like doing this at home, talk to your local butcher and tell them that you need ground beef with higher Fat: content. Also, be sure to always use freshly ground beef. The longer it's sitting in packaging, the more compressed it's getting, and compressed beef is the enemy of the perfect burger.

Once you have the right beef, form it into loose balls about 1/3 of a pound. Don't work it too much, and don't press it together, as you want the balls to just barely hold together. Light your griddle and turn the burners to medium heat. You might think that burgers cook best at high heat, but this is wrong. You want to give your burgers time to let their Fat: render and develop a nice flavorful sear. If you cook too fast, you'll end up with overcooked burgers that are chewy inside. Drizzle a little vegetable oil on the griddle and place the ball on the griddle. Using a grill weight, press down to "smash" the burger as flat as you'd like. Don't reshape it, just let it press onto the griddle and sprinkle with salt. Use your thumb to make an indentation in the center of the burger so that it stays flat when the first side has developed a nice sear, flip, season with salt and cook for an equal amount of time. This way, your burger will have the time to render its Fat: and reabsorb it as it cooks. When you've reached the temperature you prefer, remove it from the griddle and allow it to rest for five minutes. Top it however you'd like and enjoy what will be the best burger you've ever had.

Breakfast Recipes

Brioche with Cinnamon French Toast

 Prep Time 5 min   **Cook Time** 10 min   **Servings** 5

1. In a bowl, whisk the eggs well. Mix in half and half, cinnamon, and almond extract. Soak bread in the egg batter for 5 minutes.

2. Preheat the griddle pan on medium heat, for 3-4 minutes. Melt 2 tbsp butter onto the pan. Cook the French toast to the desired doneness. Repeat until all are cooked. Serve with maple syrup.

10 eggs
¾ cup half and half
2 teaspoons cinnamon
1 teaspoon almond extract
1/4 cup maple syrup, to serve
1 loaf brioche bread, sliced

Nutrition: Calories: 200, Carbs: 8 g, Fat: 5 g, Protein: 2 g

Peanut Butter Grape Jelly Pancake

 Prep Time 15 min   **Cook Time** 25 min   **Servings** 6

Pancakes:
2 eggs
1 1/2 cups whole milk 1/2 cup smooth peanut butter
1 1/4 cups pancake mix
Peanut Butter Cream:
1/2 cup smooth peanut butter
1 (8-oz.) container whipped topping

Grape Syrup:
1/4 cup grape jelly
1/2 cup maple syrup

1. Preheat the griddle pan over medium heat. Make pancake batter: Beat together the egg and milk. Add the peanut butter and beat until smooth. Mix in the pancake mix.

2. For your peanut buttercream, mix the peanut butter plus whipped topping. For the grape syrup, combine the jelly and syrup. Microwave until melted, about 20 seconds. Mix to combine.

3. Ladle a half cup of the pancake batter onto the pan. Cook until golden brown, about 2 minutes per side. Continue until all batter is used up.

4. Stack the pancakes, spreading a smear of the peanut buttercream between each pancake. Spry with the grape syrup before serving.

Nutrition: Calories: 320, Carbs: 36 g, Fat: 17 g, Protein: 10 g

Spicy Bacon Burrito with Potato and Avocado

 Prep Time 5 min   **Cook Time** 15 min   **Servings** 4

4 eggs
4 strips bacon
1 russet potato, large, peeled, and cut into small cubes
1 red bell pepper
1/2 yellow onion
1 ripe avocado, sliced
2 tablespoon hot sauce
2 large flour tortillas
Vegetable oil

Nutrition: Calories: 541, Carbs: 33 g, Fat: 20 g, Protein: 25 g

1. Preheat the griddle to medium-high heat on one side and medium heat on the other side. Brush with vegetable oil and add the bacon to the medium heat side and peppers and onions to the medium-high side.
2. When the bacon finishes cooking, place it on paper towels and chop it into small pieces. Add the potatoes to the bacon Fat: on the griddle. Cook the potatoes until softened.
3. Add the eggs to the vegetable side and cook until firm. Place the ingredients onto the tortillas and top with slices of avocado and a tablespoon of hot sauce. Fold the tortillas and enjoy.

1 cup vanilla ice cream, melted
3 eggs
1 teaspoon vanilla extract
The ground cinnamon, as needed
8 slices of Texas toast/other thick-cut bread
Cooking oil, as needed

French Toast with Melted Vanilla Ice Cream

 Prep Time 5 min   **Cook Time** 5 min   **Servings** 8

1. Mix the melted ice cream, eggs, vanilla extract, and cinnamon in a bowl until frothy.
2. Set the griddle to medium-high heat, then coat the surface using oil. Dip each side of the bread into your prepared batter.
3. Put the bread on your griddle, then cook within 3 to 4 minutes on each side. Repeat with the remaining fixings, and serve.

Nutrition: Calories: 287, Carbs: 43 g, Fat: 15 g, Protein: 45 g

Spicy Egg Scrambled

 Prep Time 3 min   **Cook Time** 10 min   **Servings** 2

4 eggs
2 tablespoons cilantro, chopped
1/3 cup heavy cream
1 tomato, diced
3 tablespoons butter
1 Serrano chili pepper, chopped
2 tablespoons scallions, sliced
1/4 teaspoons pepper
1/2 teaspoons salt

1. Preheat the griddle to medium heat.
2. Melt butter on top of the hot griddle.
3. Add tomato and chili pepper and sauté for 2 minutes.
4. In a bowl, whisk eggs with cilantro, cream, pepper, and salt.
5. Pour egg mixture over tomato and chili pepper and stir until egg is set.
6. Garnish with scallions and serve.

Nutrition: Calories: 355, Fat: 33 g, Carbs: 3 g, Protein: 12 g

Gruyere Omelet with Bacon

 Prep Time 15 min   **Cook Time** 10 min   **Servings** 6

6 eggs, beaten
6 strips bacon
1/4 pound Gruyere, shredded
1 teaspoon black pepper
1 teaspoon salt
1 tablespoon chives, finely chopped
Vegetable oil

Nutrition: Calories: 249, Carbs: 2 g, Fat: 19 g, Protein: 24 g

1. Add salt to the beaten eggs and set aside for 10 minutes. Heat your griddle to medium heat and add the bacon strips.
2. Cook until most of the Fat: has been rendered, but bacon is still flexible. Remove the bacon from the griddle and place it on paper towels. Once the bacon has drained, chop it into small pieces.
3. Add the eggs to the griddle in two even pools. Cook until the bottom of the eggs starts to firm up.
4. Add the gruyere to the eggs and cook until the cheese has started to melt and the eggs are just starting to brown.
5. Add the bacon pieces and use a spatula to turn one half of the omelet onto the other half. Remove from the griddle, season with pepper and chives, and serve.

2 eggs, lightly beaten
2 tablespoons fresh basil, chopped
1 tablespoon olive oil
1/2 tomato, chopped
Pepper, to taste
Salt, to taste

Scrambled Egg with Tomato and Basil

 Prep Time 5 min   **Cook Time** 15 min   **Servings** 2

1. Preheat the griddle to medium heat. Add oil on top of the griddle. Add tomatoes and cook until softened.
2. Whisk eggs with basil, pepper, and salt. Pour egg mixture on top of tomatoes and cook until eggs are set. Serve and enjoy.

Nutrition: Calories: 125, Fat: 12 g, Carbs: 1 g, Protein: 5.8 g

17

---

6 eggs
3 oz cherry tomatoes, cut in halves
1 tablespoon fresh basil
5 oz mozzarella cheese, sliced
Pepper
Salt

Caprese Omelet

 Prep Time 5 min   **Cook Time** 10 min   **Servings** 6

1. Preheat the griddle to medium-low heat
2. Whisk eggs in a bowl with pepper and salt. Stir in basil.
3. Spray griddle top with cooking spray.
4. Add tomatoes to the hot griddle top and sauté for a few minutes.
5. Pour egg mixture on top of tomatoes and wait until eggs are slightly firm.
6. Add mozzarella cheese slices on top and let the omelet set.
7. Servings and enjoy.

Nutrition: Calories: 515, Fat: 40 g, Carbs: 5 g, Protein: 37 g

Scrambled Egg with Black Beans and Chorizo

 Prep Time 5 min **Cook Time** 10 min **Servings** 8

8 eggs, beaten
1 pound Chorizo
1/2 yellow onion
1 cup cooked black beans
1/2 cup green chilies
1/2 cup jack cheese
1/4 cup green onion, chopped
1/2 teaspoon black pepper
Vegetable oil

1. Preheat a griddle to medium heat. Brush your griddle using vegetable oil and add the chorizo to one side and the onions to the other side.
2. When the onion has softened, combine it with the chorizo and add the beans and chilies. Add the eggs, cheese, and green onion and cook until eggs have reached desired firmness.
3. Remove the scramble from the griddle and season with black pepper before serving.

Nutrition: Calories: 129, Carbs: 2 g, Fat: 7 g, Protein: 10 g

---

Cheesy Bacon and Egg Sandwich

 Prep Time 5 min **Cook Time** 20 min **Servings** 4

4 large eggs
8 strips of bacon
4 slices of Cheddar or American cheese
8 slices of sourdough bread
2 tablespoons butter
2 tablespoons vegetable oil

1. Heat your griddle to medium heat and place the strips of bacon on one side. Cook until just slightly crispy.
2. When the bacon is nearly finished, place the oil on the other side of the griddle and crack with eggs onto the griddle. Cook them either sunny side up or over medium.
3. Butter one side of each slice of your bread and place the butter side down on the griddle.
4. Place a slice of cheese on 4 of the slices of bread and when the cheese has just started to melt, and the eggs are finished, stack the eggs on the bread. Add the bacon to the sandwiches and place the other slice of bread on top. Serve immediately.

Nutrition: Calories: 310, Carbs: 7 g, Fat: 22 g, Protein: 19 g

---

Griddled Fruit Salad with Honey-Lime Glaze

 Prep Time 15 min **Cook Time** 5 min **Servings** 2

1/2 pound strawberries, washed, hulled, and halved
1 (9 oz.) can pineapple chunks, drained, juice reserved
2 peaches, pitted and sliced
6 tablespoons honey, divided
1 tablespoon freshly squeezed lime juice

1. Preheat your griddle to medium-high.
2. While the unit is preheating, combine the strawberries, pineapple, and peaches in a large bowl with 3 tablespoons of honey. Toss to coat evenly.
3. Place the fruit on the griddle. Gently press the fruit down. Cook for 4 minutes without flipping.
4. Meanwhile, in a small bowl, combine the remaining 3 tablespoons of honey, lime juice, and 1 tablespoon of reserved pineapple juice.
5. When cooking is complete, place the fruit in a large bowl and toss it with the honey mixture. Serve immediately.

Nutrition: Calories: 178, Fat: 1 g, Carbs: 47 g, Protein: 2 g

Onion, Pepper, and Mushroom Frittata

 Prep Time 10 min   **Cook Time** 10 min   **Servings** 4

1. Preheat the griddle to medium-high.
2. In a medium bowl, whisk together the eggs and milk. Season with salt and pepper. Add the bell pepper, onion, mushrooms, and cheese. Mix until well combined.
3. Pour the egg mixture into the Ninja Multi-Purpose Pan or baking pan, spreading evenly.
4. Place the pan directly on the griddle and cook for 10 minutes, or until lightly golden.

4 large eggs
1/4 cup whole milk
Sea salt
Freshly ground black pepper
1/2 bell pepper, seeded and diced
1/2 onion, chopped
4 cremini mushrooms, sliced
1/2 cup shredded Cheddar cheese

Nutrition: Calories: 153, Fat: 10 g, Carbs: 5 g, Protein: 11 g

Fried Pickles

 Prep Time 20 min   **Cook Time** 10 min   **Servings** 8

20 dill pickle slices
1/4 cup all-purpose flour
1/8 teaspoons baking powder
3 tablespoons beer or seltzer water
1/8 teaspoons sea salt
2 tablespoons water, plus more if needed
2 tablespoons cornstarch
1-1/2 cups panko breadcrumbs
1 teaspoon paprika
1 teaspoon garlic powder
1/4 teaspoons cayenne pepper
2 tablespoons canola oil, divided

1. Preheat the griddle to medium-high.
2. Pat the pickle slices dry and place them on a dry plate in the freezer.
3. In a medium bowl, stir together the flour, baking powder, beer, salt, and water. The batter should be the consistency of the cake batter. If it is too thick, add more water, 1 teaspoon at a time.
4. Place the cornstarch in a small shallow bowl.
5. In a separate large shallow bowl, combine the breadcrumbs, paprika, garlic powder, and cayenne pepper.
6. Remove the pickles from the freezer. Dredge each one in cornstarch.
7. Tap off any excess, then coat in the batter. Lastly, coat evenly with the bread crumb mixture.
8. Set on the griddle top and gently brush the breaded pickles with 1 tablespoon of oil. Cook for 5 minutes.
9. After 5 minutes, turn and gently brush the pickles with the remaining 1 tablespoon of oil and resume cooking. When cooking is complete, serve immediately.

Nutrition: Calories: 296, Fat: 10 g, Carbs: 44 g, Protein: 7 g

Classic Buttermilk Pancakes

 Prep Time 15 min   **Cook Time** 25 min   **Servings** 2

1. In a large bowl, combine the flour, sugar, baking soda, baking powder, and salt.
2. Stir in the buttermilk, eggs, and butter, and mix until combined but not smooth.
3. Heat your griddle to medium heat and add a small amount of oil. Using a paper towel, spread the oil over the griddle in a very thin layer.
4. Use a ladle to pour the batter onto the griddle allowing a few inches between pancakes.
5. When the surface of the pancakes is bubbly, flip and cook for a few additional minutes, remove the pancakes from the griddle and serve immediately with butter and maple syrup.

2 cups all-purpose flour
3 tablespoons sugar
1-1/2 teaspoons baking powder
1-1/2 teaspoons baking soda
1-1/4 teaspoons salt
2-1/2 cup buttermilk
2 eggs
3 tablespoons unsalted butter, melted
2 tablespoons vegetable oil

Nutrition: Calories: 432, Fat: 13 g, Carbs: 65 g, Protein: 14 g

Fluffy Blueberry Pancakes

 Prep Time 5 min   **Cook Time** 10 min   **Servings** 2

1. In a bowl, combine the milk and vinegar. Set aside for two minutes.
2. In a large bowl, combine the flour, sugar, baking powder, baking soda, and salt. Stir in the milk, egg, blueberries, and melted butter. Mix until combined but not smooth.
3. Heat your griddle to medium heat and add a little butter. Pour the pancakes onto the griddle and cook until one side is golden brown.
4. Flip the pancakes and cook until the other side is golden.
5. Remove the pancakes from the griddle and serve with warm maple syrup.

1 cup flour
3/4 cup milk
2 tablespoons white vinegar
2 tablespoons sugar
1 teaspoon baking powder
1/2 teaspoons baking soda
1/2 teaspoons salt
1 egg
2 tablespoons butter, melted
1 cup fresh blueberries
Butter for cooking

Nutrition: Calories: 499, Fat: 16 g, Carbs: 76 g, Protein: 12 g

Griddled Pizza with Eggs and Greens

 Prep Time 15 min Cook Time 25 min Servings 4

2 tablespoons all-purpose flour, plus more as needed
1/2 store-bought pizza dough (about 8 ounces)
1 tablespoon canola oil, divided
1 cup fresh ricotta cheese
4 large eggs
Sea salt
Freshly ground black pepper
4 cups arugula, torn
1 tablespoon extra-virgin olive oil
1 teaspoon freshly squeezed lemon juice
2 tablespoons grated Parmesan cheese

1. Preheat the griddle to medium-high.
2. Dust a clean work surface with flour. Place the dough on the floured surface, and roll it into a 9-inch round of even thickness. Dust your rolling pin and work surface with additional flour, as needed, to ensure the dough does not stick.
3. Brush the surface of the rolled-out dough evenly with 1/2 tablespoon of canola oil. Flip the dough over and brush with the remaining 1/2 tablespoon of oil. Poke the dough with a fork 5 or 6 times across its surface to prevent air pockets from forming during cooking.
4. Place the dough on the griddle and cook for 4 minutes.
5. After 4 minutes, flip the dough, then spoon teaspoons of ricotta cheese across the surface of the dough, leaving a 1-inch border around the edges.
6. Crack one egg into a ramekin or small bowl. This way, you can easily remove any shell that may break into the egg and keep the yolk intact. Imagine the dough is split into four quadrants. Pour one egg into each. Repeat with the remaining 3 eggs. Season the pizza with salt and pepper.
7. Continue cooking for the remaining 3 to 4 minutes until the egg whites are firm.
8. Meanwhile, in a medium bowl, toss together the arugula, oil, and lemon juice, and season with salt and pepper. Transfer the pizza to a cutting board and let it cool. Top it with the arugula mixture, drizzle with olive oil, if desired, and sprinkle with Parmesan cheese.
9. Cut into pieces and serve.

Nutrition: Calories: 432, Fat: 13 g, Carbs: 65 g, Protein: 14 g

---

Simple French Crepes

 Prep Time 15 min Cook Time 5 min Servings 2

1 1/4 cups flour
3/4 cup whole milk
1/2 cup water
2 eggs
3 tablespoons unsalted butter, melted
1 teaspoon vanilla
2 tablespoon sugar

1. In a large bowl, add all the ingredients and mix with a whisk. Make sure the batter is smooth. Rest for 1 hour.
2. Heat your Outdoor Griddle to medium heat and add a thin layer of butter. Add about 1/4 cup of the batter. Using a crepe spreading tool, form your crepe and cook for 1-2 minutes. Use your Crepe Spatula and flip. Cook for another minute.
3. Top with Nutella and strawberries for a sweet crepe, or top with scrambled eggs and black forest ham for a savory crepe.

Nutrition: Calories: 303, Fat: 13 g, Carbs: 38 g, Protein: 8 g

Bacon and Gruyere Omelet

 Prep Time 15 min   **Cook Time** 20 min   **Servings** 6

1. Add salt to the beaten eggs and set aside for 10 minutes.

2. Heat your griddle to medium heat and add the bacon strips. Cook until most of the Fat: has been rendered, but bacon is still flexible. Remove the bacon from the griddle and place it on paper towels.

3. Once the bacon has drained, chop it into small pieces.

4. Add the eggs to the griddle in two even pools. Cook until the bottom of the eggs starts to firm up. Add the gruyere to the eggs and cook until the cheese has started to melt and the eggs are just starting to brown.

5. Add the bacon pieces and use a spatula to turn one half of the omelet onto the other half.

6. Remove from the griddle, season with pepper and chives, and serve.

6 eggs, beaten
6 strips bacon
1/4 pound gruyere, shredded
1 teaspoon black pepper
1 teaspoon salt
1 tablespoon chives, finely chopped
Vegetable oil

Nutrition: Calories: 734, Fat: 55 g, Carbs: 3 g, Protein: 55 g

Classic Denver Omelet

 Prep Time 20 min   **Cook Time** 15 min   **Servings** 6

1. Heat your griddle to medium heat and place the butter onto the griddle.

2. Add the ham, onion, and pepper to the butter and cook until the vegetables have just softened.

3. Beat the eggs in a large bowl and add a pinch of salt and cayenne pepper.

4. Split the vegetables into portions on the griddle and add half of the eggs to each portion. Cook until the eggs have begun to firm up, and then add the cheese to each omelet.

5. Fold the omelets over and remove them from the griddle. Serve immediately.

6 large eggs
1/4 cup country ham, diced
1/4 cup yellow onion, finely chopped
1/4 cup green bell pepper, chopped
2/3 cup Cheddar cheese, shredded
1/4 teaspoon cayenne pepper
Salt and black pepper
2 tablespoons butter

Nutrition: Calories: 507, Fat: 40 g, Carbs: 5 g, Protein: 31 g

Griddled Cinnamon Toast with Berries and Whipped Cream

 Prep Time 15 min **Cook Time** 15 min **Servings** 4

1 (15-ounce) can of full-Fat: coconut milk, refrigerated overnight
1/2 tablespoon powdered sugar
1-1/2 teaspoons vanilla extract, divided
1 cup halved strawberries
1 tablespoon maple syrup, plus more for garnish
1 tablespoon brown sugar, divided
3/4 cup lite coconut milk
2 large eggs
1/2 teaspoon ground cinnamon
2 tablespoons unsalted butter, at room temperature
4 slices of Challah bread

1. Turn the chilled can of full-Fat: coconut milk upside down (do not shake the can), open the bottom, and pour out the liquid coconut water. Scoop the remaining solid coconut cream into a medium bowl. Using an electric hand mixer, whip the cream for 3 to 5 minutes, until soft peaks form.
2. Add the powdered sugar and 1/2 teaspoon of the vanilla to the coconut cream, and whip it again until creamy. Place the bowl in the refrigerator.
3. Preheat the griddle to medium-high. While the unit is preheating, combine the strawberries with the maple syrup and toss to coat evenly.
4. Sprinkle evenly with 1/2 tablespoon of the brown sugar.
5. In a large shallow bowl, whisk together the lite coconut milk, eggs, the remaining 1 teaspoon of vanilla, and cinnamon.
6. Place the strawberries on the griddle. Gently press the fruit down. Cook for 4 minutes without flipping.
7. Meanwhile, butter each slice of bread on both sides. Place one slice in the egg mixture and let it soak for 1 minute. Flip the slice over and soak it for another minute. Repeat with the remaining bread slices. Sprinkle each side of the toast with the remaining 1/2 tablespoon of brown sugar.
8. After 4 minutes, remove the strawberries from the griddle and set them aside. Decrease the temperature to medium-low. Place the bread on the griddle and cook for 4 to 6 minutes, until golden and caramelized. Check often to ensure the desired doneness.
9. Place the toast on a plate and top with the strawberries and whipped coconut cream.
10. Drizzle with maple syrup, if desired.

Nutrition: Calories: 386, Fat: 19 g, Carbs: 49 g, Protein: 7 g

23

Almond Pancakes

 Prep Time 5 min   **Cook Time** 5 min  **Servings** 2

1 egg
1/2 cup almond flour
1/2 teaspoon baking powder
1/2 tablespoon heavy whipping cream
1 1/2 tablespoons Swerve

1. Preheat the griddle to medium-low heat.
2. In a bowl, mix almond flour, baking powder, sweetener, and salt.
3. In another bowl, whisk egg and heavy whipping cream.
4. Add dry ingredients to the wet and mix well.
5. Spray griddle top with cooking spray.
6. Drop batter onto the hot griddle top.
7. Cook pancakes until lightly golden brown from both sides.
8. Servings and enjoy.

Nutrition: Calories: 90, Fat: 7 g, Carbs: 13 g, Protein: 4 g

Classic French Toast

 Prep Time 10 min   **Cook Time** 5 min   **Servings** 6

1. Heat your griddle to medium heat.
2. In a large bowl, combine the eggs, cream, sugar, cinnamon, and salt. Mix well until smooth.
3. Lightly grease the griddle with butter or vegetable oil.
4. Dip each slice of bread in the mixture until well saturated with egg, then place onto the griddle.
5. When the French toast has begun to brown, flip and cook until the other side has browned as well—about four minutes. Remove the French toast from the griddle, dust with powdered sugar, and serve with warm maple syrup.

6 eggs, beaten
1/4 cup "half and half" or heavy cream
8 slices of thick-cut white or sourdough bread
2 tablespoons sugar
1 tablespoon cinnamon
1 teaspoon salt - butter
Powdered sugar
Maple syrup

Nutrition: Calories: 332, Fat: 10 g, Carbs: 44 g, Protein: 16 g

---

Cauliflower Fritters

 Prep Time 5 min   **Cook Time** 10 min   **Servings** 1

1. Add cauliflower florets to a large pot.
2. Pour enough water to cover the cauliflower florets. Bring to boil for 8-10 minutes.
3. Drain cauliflower well and transfer it to a food processor, and process until it looks like rice.
4. Transfer cauliflower rice into a large bowl.
5. Add remaining ingredients except for butter to the bowl and stir to combine.
6. Preheat the griddle to medium heat.
7. Melt butter onto the hot griddle top.
8. Make small patties from cauliflower mixture and place on hot griddle top and cook for 3-4 minutes on each side or until lightly golden brown.
9. Servings and enjoy.

2 eggs
1 large head cauliflower, cut into florets
1 tablespoon butter
1/2 teaspoons turmeric
1 tablespoon nutrition yeast
2/3 cup almond flour
1/4 teaspoon black pepper
1/2 teaspoon salt

Nutrition: Calories: 155, Fat: 10 g, Carbs: 11 g, Protein: 8 g

Bacon Egg and Cheese Sandwich

 Prep Time 5 min   **Cook Time** 20 min   **Servings** 4

1. Heat your griddle to medium heat and place the strips of bacon on one side. Cook until just slightly crispy.
2. When the bacon is nearly finished, place the oil on the other side of the griddle and crack with eggs onto the griddle. Cook them either sunny side up or over medium.
3. Butter one side of each slice of bread and place the butter side down on the griddle. Place a slice of cheese on 4 of the slices of bread and when the cheese has just started to melt, and the eggs are finished, stack the eggs on the bread.
4. Add the bacon to the sandwiches and place the other slice of bread on top. Serve immediately.

4 large eggs
8 strips of bacon
4 slices of Cheddar or American cheese
8 slices of sourdough bread
2 tablespoons butter
2 tablespoons vegetable oil

Nutrition: Calories: 699, Fat: 48 g, Carbs: 38 g, Protein: 29 g

French Toast Sticks

 Prep Time 10 min   **Cook Time** 15 min   **Servings** 1

1. Preheat the griddle to medium-low heat.
2. In a bowl, whisk eggs with cinnamon, vanilla, and milk.
3. Spray griddle top with cooking spray.
4. Dip each bread piece into the egg mixture and coat well.
5. Place coated bread pieces onto the hot griddle top and cook until golden brown from both sides.
6. Servings and enjoy.

2 eggs
4 bread slices, cut each bread slice into 3 pieces vertically
2/3 cup milk
1/4 teaspoons ground cinnamon
1 teaspoon vanilla

Nutrition: Calories: 166, Fat: 7 g, Carbs: 14 g, Protein: 10 g

Healthy Oatmeal Pancake

 Prep Time 5 min   **Cook Time** 20 min   **Servings** 6

6 egg whites
1 cup steel-cut oats
1/4 teaspoons vanilla
1 cup Greek yogurt
1/2 teaspoons baking powder
1 teaspoon liquid stevia
1/4 teaspoons cinnamon

1. Preheat the griddle to medium-low heat.
2. Add oats to a blender and blend until a fine powder is a form.
3. Add remaining ingredients into the blender and blend until well combined.
4. Spray griddle top with cooking spray.
5. Pour 1/4 cup batter onto the hot griddle top.
6. Cook pancake until golden brown from both sides.
7. Servings and enjoy.

Nutrition: Calories: 295, Fat: 4 g, Carbs: 37 g, Protein: 23 g a

Simple Cheese Sandwich

   Prep Time 5 min   **Cook Time** 5 min   **Servings** 1

2 bread slices
2 teaspoons butter
2 cheese slices

1. Preheat the griddle to medium-low heat.
2. Place cheese slices on top of one bread slice and cover cheese with another bread slice.
3. Spread butter on top of both bread slices.
4. Place sandwich on hot griddle top and cook until golden brown or until cheese is melted.
5. Servings and enjoy.

Nutrition: Calories: 340, Fat: 26 g, Carbs: 9 g, Protein: 15 g

---

Tomato Scrambled Egg

   Prep Time 4 min   **Cook Time** 5 min   **Servings** 2

2 eggs, lightly beaten
2 tablespoons fresh basil, chopped
1 tablespoon olive oil
1/2 tomato, chopped
Pepper
Salt

1. Preheat the griddle to medium heat.
2. Add oil on top of the griddle.
3. Add tomatoes and cook until softened.
4. Whisk eggs with basil, pepper, and salt.
5. Pour egg mixture on top of tomatoes and cook until eggs are set.
6. Servings and enjoy.

Nutrition: Calories: 125, Fat: 12 g, Carbs: 1 g, Protein: 6 g

---

Pumpkin Pancake

   Prep Time 10 min   **Cook Time** 20 min   **Servings** 4

4 eggs
1/2 teaspoons cinnamon
1/2 cup pumpkin puree
1 cup almond flour
2 teaspoons liquid stevia
1 teaspoon baking powder

1. Preheat the griddle to medium-low heat.
2. In a bowl, mix almond flour, stevia, baking powder, cinnamon, pumpkin puree, and eggs until well combined.
3. Spray griddle top with cooking spray.
4. Drop batter onto the hot griddle top.
5. Cook pancakes until lightly golden brown from both sides.
6. Servings and enjoy.

Nutrition: Calories: 235, Fat: 18 g, Carbs: 9 g, Protein: 12 g

Easy Banana Pancakes

 Prep Time 10 min

 Cook Time 5 min

 Servings 1

2 eggs
2 tablespoons vanilla Protein: powder
1 large banana, mashed
1/8 teaspoons baking powder

1. Preheat the griddle to medium-low heat.
2. Meanwhile, add all ingredients into the bowl and mix well until combined.
3. Spray griddle top with cooking spray.
4. Pour 3 tablespoons of batter onto the hot griddle top to make a pancake.
5. Cook pancake until lightly browned from both sides.
6. Servings and enjoy.

Nutrition: Calories: 79, Fat: 2 g, Carbs: 5 g, Protein: 11 g

Easy Cheese Omelet

 Prep Time 12 min

 Cook Time 18 min

 Servings 3

6 eggs
7 oz Cheddar cheese, shredded
3 oz butter
Pepper
Salt

1. In a bowl, whisk together eggs, half cheese, pepper, and salt.
2. Preheat the griddle to medium heat.
3. Melt butter on the hot griddle top.
4. Once butter is melted, then pour the egg mixture onto the griddle top and cook until set.
5. Add remaining cheese fold and serve.

Nutrition: Calories: 892, Fat: 80 g, Carbs: 2 g, Protein: 42 g

Toad in a Hole

 Prep Time 5 min

 Cook Time 10 min

 Servings 2

4 slices of white, wheat, or sourdough bread
4 eggs
2 tablespoons butter
Salt and black pepper

1. Preheat the griddle to medium heat, and add the butter, spreading it around.
2. Cut a hole in the center of each slice of bread.
3. Place the slices of bread on the griddle and crack an egg into the holes in each slice of bread.
4. Cook until the bread begins to brown, then flip and cook until the egg whites are firm.
5. Remove from the griddle and season with salt and black pepper before serving.

Nutrition: Calories: 206, Fat: 10 g, Carbs: 18 g, Protein: 9 g

Chocolate Pancake

 Prep Time 10 min   **Cook Time** 5 min   **Servings** 1

1. In a bowl, mix ground flaxseed, baking powder, erythritol, cocoa powder, spices, and salt.
2. Add eggs and stir well.
3. Add water and stir until batter is well combined.
4. Preheat the griddle to medium-low heat.
5. Spray griddle top with cooking spray.
6. Pour a large spoonful of batter on a hot griddle top and make a pancake.
7. Cook pancake for 3-4 minutes on each side.
8. Servings and enjoy.

2 eggs
1/2 teaspoons baking powder
2 tablespoons erythritol
1 1/2 tablespoons cocoa powder
1/4 cup ground flaxseed
2 tablespoons water
1 teaspoon nutmeg
1 teaspoon cinnamon
1/4 teaspoons salt

Nutrition: Calories: 138, Fat: 12 g, Carbs: 11 g, Protein: 4 g

Spinach Pancakes

 Prep Time 7 min   **Cook Time** 20 min   **Servings** 4

1. In a bowl, whisk eggs with coconut milk until frothy.
2. Mix all dry ingredients and add in the egg mixture and whisk until smooth.
3. Add spinach and stir well.
4. Preheat the griddle to medium-low heat.
5. Spray griddle top with cooking spray.
6. Pour 3-4 tablespoons of batter onto the hot griddle top and make a round pancake.
7. Cook pancake until lightly golden brown from both sides.
8. Servings and enjoy.

4 eggs
1 cup coconut milk
1/4 cup chia seeds
1 cup spinach, chopped
1/2 teaspoons black pepper
1/2 teaspoons ground nutmeg
1 teaspoon baking soda
1/2 cup coconut flour
1/2 teaspoons salt

Nutrition: Calories: 111, Fat: 7 g, Carbs: 5 g, Protein: 6 g

Burger Recipes

1/3 cup finely crushed corn tortilla chips
1 egg, beaten
1/4 cup salsa
1/3 cup shredded pepper Jack cheese
Pinch salt
Freshly ground black pepper
1 pound ground turkey
1 tablespoon olive oil
1 teaspoon paprika

Tex-Mex Turkey Burgers

 Prep Time
5 min   **Cook Time**
16 min   **Servings**
1

1. Preparing the Ingredients. In a medium bowl, combine the tortilla chips, egg, salsa, cheese, salt, and pepper, and mix well.
2. Add the turkey and mix gently but thoroughly with clean hands.
3. Form the meat mixture into patties about 1/2 inch thick.
4. Brush the patties on both sides with olive oil and sprinkle with paprika.
5. Turn the control knob to the high position. When the griddle is hot, place the burgers and cook for 14 to 16 minutes or until the meat registers at least 165°F.
6.

Nutrition: Calories: 354, Fat: 21 g, Protein: 36 g

11/2 pounds boneless lamb shoulder or leg or good-quality ground lamb
1 tablespoon chopped fresh oregano
1 teaspoon salt
1 teaspoon black pepper
1 tablespoon minced garlic
1/2 cup Greek yogurt
1 tablespoon olive oil, plus more for brushing
1 tablespoon red wine vinegar
2 tablespoons crumbled feta cheese
4 or 5 ciabatta rolls, split, or 8–10 slider buns (like potato or dinner rolls)
Thinly sliced cucumbers for serving

Nutrition: Calories: 519, Fat: 53 g, Protein: 83 g

Tzatziki Lamb Burgers

 Prep Time
15 min   **Cook Time**
30 min   **Servings**
8

1. Preparing the Ingredients.
2. Put the lamb, oregano, salt, pepper, and garlic in a food processor and pulse until coarsely ground—finer than chopped, but not much. (If you're using pre-ground meat, put it in a bowl with the seasonings and work them together gently with your hands.) Take a bit of the mixture and fry it up to taste for seasoning; adjust if necessary. Handling the meat as little as possible to avoid compressing it, shape the mixture lightly into 4 or 5 burgers or 8 to 10 sliders. Refrigerate the burgers until you're ready to cook; if you make them several hours in advance, cover them with plastic wrap.
3. Whisk the yogurt, oil, and vinegar together in a small bowl until smooth. Stir in the feta. Taste and adjust the seasoning with salt and pepper.
4. Bring the griddle to high heat. When the griddle is hot, place the burgers and cook for 11 minutes.
5. Transfer the burgers to a plate. Brush the cut sides of the rolls lightly with oil and toast directly over the griddle for 1 to 2 minutes. Top with a burger, then several slices of cucumber, a dollop of the sauce, and the other half of the roll. Serve with the remaining sauce on the side.

Beef Burgers

Prep Time	Cook Time	Servings
15 min	5 min	4

11/4 pounds lean ground beef
1 small onion, minced
1/4 cup teriyaki sauce
3 tablespoons Italian-flavored bread crumbs
2 tablespoons grated Parmesan cheese
1 teaspoon salt
1 teaspoon freshly ground black pepper
3 tablespoons sweet pickle relish
4 Kaiser rolls, toasted

1. Preparing the Ingredients.
2. Put the beef in a medium bowl and add the onion, teriyaki sauce, bread crumbs, Parmesan cheese, salt, and pepper. Using a fork, mix the seasonings into the meat and then form the mixture into 4 patties, each about 1 inch thick.
3. Bring the griddle to high heat, when the griddle is hot, place the burgers and cook for 4 minutes without flipping. Remove the burgers and cover to keep warm. Top each burger with a spoonful of sweet pickle relish before sandwiching between a bun. Serve immediately.

Nutrition: Calories: 519, Fat: 23 g, Protein: 33 g

Chipotle Burgers with Avocado

Prep Time	Cook Time	Servings
5 min	5 min	4

11/4 pounds lean ground beef
2 tablespoons chipotle puree
1/2 teaspoon salt
1/4 teaspoon freshly ground black pepper
4 slices of Cheddar cheese (about 4 ounces)
1 avocado, halved, pitted, and sliced
1/4 head iceberg lettuce, shredded
4 hamburger buns, toasted

1. Preparing the Ingredients.
2. Put the beef in a medium bowl and add the chipotle puree, salt, and pepper. Using a fork, mix the seasonings into the meat and then, with your hands, form the mixture into 4 patties, each about 1 inch thick.
3. Turn the control knob to the high position, when the griddle is hot, place the burgers and cook for 4 minutes without Flipping. Top each burger with a slice of cheese and cook for 1 minute more until the cheese melts. Remove the burgers and cover to keep warm.
4. Top each burger with a few slices of avocado and some shredded lettuce before sandwiching between a bun.
5. Chipotle Puree: Put canned chipotles and their liquid in a blender or food processor and process until smooth. The puree can be covered with plastic wrap and refrigerated for up to 2 weeks. This stuff is hot-hot-hot, so a little goes a long way. I use it in meat marinades and dips. The puree is sold in some grocery stores, in the ethnic mark.

Nutrition: Calories: 590, Fat: 38 g, Carbs: 0 g, Protein: 37 g

Caesar Salad Poultry Burgers

1/4 cup mayonnaise
2 cloves garlic, 1 minced, 1 peeled, and left whole
2 oil-packed anchovy fillets, drained and mashed
2 tablespoons freshly grated Parmesan cheese
1 tablespoon fresh lemon juice
1/2 teaspoon Worcestershire sauce
11/2 pounds ground chicken or turkey
Good-quality vegetable oil for oiling the grates
4 ciabatta rolls, split, or 8–10 slider buns
Good-quality olive oil for brushing the rolls
1 leaves heart of romaine, trimmed

Prep Time	Cook Time	Servings
10 min	8 min	8

1. Preparing the Ingredients.
2. Line a baking sheet with wax paper. Whisk the mayonnaise, minced garlic, anchovies, Parmesan, lemon juice, and Worcestershire together in a small bowl until smooth. Put the chicken in a medium bowl and add 2 tablespoons of the dressing. Cover and refrigerate the remaining dressing. Work the dressing into the chicken with your hands gently but completely. Form the mixture into 4 burgers ¾ to 1 inch thick. Put them on the prepared pan, cover, and refrigerate until firm, at least 1 hour.
3. Turn the control knob to the high position, when the griddle is hot, brush the cut sides of the rolls with olive oil. Brush the burgers with oil on both sides, and put them on the griddle. Carefully turn once with two spatulas, until browned on the outside and no longer pink in the center, 5 to 7 minutes per side.
4. For the last couple of minutes, toast the rolls on the griddle, and cut the side down. To serve, rub the cut side of the top of each roll with the whole garlic clove. Put a burger on the bottom half, add a dollop of the remaining dressing, a leaf of romaine, and the top of the roll.

Nutrition: Calories: 734, Fat: 55 g, Carbs: 2 g, Protein: 54 g

Turkey Burger

 Prep Time 20 min **Cook Time** 4 min **Servings** 4

1 pound ground turkey
1 cup pine nuts or walnut pieces
3 tablespoons grated Parmesan cheese
2 tablespoons store-bought pesto
1/4 teaspoon salt
1/4 teaspoon freshly ground black pepper
4 whole wheat pitas
4 romaine lettuce leaves or 1 small handful of arugula
Lemon

1. Preparing the Ingredients.
2. Preheat the griddle to high.
3. Put the turkey in a medium bowl and add the pine nuts, Parmesan, pesto, salt, and pepper. Using a fork, mix the seasonings into the meat and then, with your hands, form the mixture into 4 patties, each about 1 inch thick.
4. Grill the patties for about 4 minutes until they are cooked through. Put each burger into a pita with some lettuce and a squeeze of lemon juice. Serve immediately.

Nutrition: Calories: 369, Fat: 21 g, Protein: 28 g

Nut Burgers

 Prep Time 5 min **Cook Time** 5 min **Servings** 8

1 cup raw rolled oats or cooked short-grain white or brown rice
1 cup walnuts, pecans, almonds, cashews, or other nuts
1 medium onion, cut into pieces
1 teaspoon chili powder
1 egg
2 tablespoons ketchup, miso, tomato
paste, nut butter, or tahini
Salt and pepper
Broth, soy sauce, wine, or other liquid if necessary

1. Preparing the Ingredients.
2. Put the onion in a food processor and pulse to a paste. Add the nuts and oats and pulse to chop, but not too finely. Add the ketchup, chili powder, some salt and pepper, and the egg. Process briefly; don't grind the mixture too finely.
3. Add a little liquid—water, broth, soy sauce, wine, whatever is handy—if necessary; the mixture should be moist enough to hold together without being wet. With damp hands, shape the mixture into 8 burgers; put on a platter without touching, and refrigerate for at least 1 hour.
4. Turn the control knob to the high position, when the griddle is hot, put them and cook, carefully turning once with two spatulas, until browned on the outside and no longer pink in the center, 5 to 7 minutes per side.

Nutrition: Calories: 296, Fat: 10 g, Carbs: 44 g, Protein: 7 g

Spiced Lamb Burger

 Prep Time 20 min **Cook Time** 5 min **Servings** 4

11/4 pounds lean ground lamb
1 tablespoon ground cumin
1/4 teaspoon ground cinnamon
1/2 teaspoon salt
1/2 teaspoon freshly ground black pepper
4 whole wheat pitas
1/2 medium cucumber, peeled and sliced
1/2 cup Simple Garlic Yogurt Sauce

1. Preparing the Ingredients.
2. Put the lamb in a medium bowl with the cumin, cinnamon, salt, and pepper. Using a fork, mix the seasonings into the meat and then, with your hands, form the mixture into 4 patties, each about 1 inch thick.
3. Turn the control knob to the high position, when the griddle is hot, place the burgers and cook for 5 minutes without flipping. Remove the burgers and cover to keep warm. Put a burger into each pita, stuff a few cucumber slices in there too, and spoon some of the yogurt sauce over the top. Serve immediately.

Nutrition: Calories: 90, Fat: 7 g, Carbs: 13 g, Protein: 4 g

11/2 pounds salmon fillet, skin, and any remaining pin bones removed, cut into chunks
2 teaspoons Dijon mustard
3 scallions, trimmed and chopped
1/4 cup bread crumbs (preferably fresh)
Salt and pepper
Good-quality olive oil for brushing
4 sesame hamburger buns or 8–10 slider buns (like potato or dinner rolls)
1 large tomato, cut into 4 thick slices

Nutrition: Calories: 444, Fat: 27 g, Carbs: 1 g, Protein: 47 g

Salmon Burgers

 Prep Time 10 min **Cook Time** 11 min **Servings** 4

1. Preparing the Ingredients.
2. Put about one-quarter of the salmon and the mustard in a food processor and purée into a paste. Add the rest of the salmon and pulse until chopped. Transfer to a bowl, add the scallions, bread crumbs, and a sprinkle of salt and pepper. Mix gently just enough to combine. Form into 4 burgers ¾ to 1 inch thick. Transfer to a plate, cover with plastic wrap and chill until firm, at least 2 or up to 8 hours.
3. Turn the control knob to the high position, when the griddle is hot, brush the burgers with oil on both sides, then put them on the griddle. Cook for 11 minutes.
4. After 11 minutes, check the burgers for doneness. Cooking is complete when the internal temperature reaches at least 165°F on a food thermometer. If necessary, close the hood and continue cooking for up to 2 minutes more.
5. Remove the burgers from the griddle.
6. Put the buns on the griddle, cut the side down, and toast for 1 to 2 minutes. Serve the burgers on the buns, topped with the tomato if used.

1/4 cup light sour cream
5 tablespoons prepared white horseradish
1/4 teaspoon salt
11/4 pounds lean ground beef
1/4 cup tomato sauce
2 tablespoons Worcestershire sauce
A dash or 2 of hot sauce
1 teaspoon celery salt
4 beefsteak tomato slices
4 brioche buns or hamburger buns, toasted
2 celery stalks, with leafy greens, each cut into 4 pieces

Nutrition: Calories: 447, Fat: 27 g, Protein: 35 g

Brunch Burgers

 Prep Time 25 min **Cook Time** 5 min **Servings** 4

1. Preparing the Ingredients.
2. In a small bowl, combine the sour cream, 2 tablespoons of horseradish, and the salt. Put the beef in a medium bowl and add the remaining 3 tablespoons of horseradish, tomato sauce, Worcestershire sauce, hot sauce, and celery salt. Using a fork, mix the seasonings into the meat and then, with your hands, form the mixture into 4 patties, each about 1 inch thick.
3. Turn the control knob to the high position, when the griddle is hot, place the burgers and cook for 4 minutes without flipping. Remove the burgers and cover to keep warm. Top with a tablespoon of horseradish sour cream and a tomato slice before sandwiching between a toasted bun. Serve immediately with the celery sticks.

Basil-Ginger Shrimp Burgers

 Prep Time 15 min **Cook Time** 5 min **Servings** 4

1 large clove of garlic, peeled
1 1-inch piece of fresh ginger, peeled and sliced
11/2 pounds shrimp, peeled (and deveined if you like)
1/2 cup lightly packed fresh basil leaves
1/4 cup roughly chopped shallots, scallions, or red onion
Salt and pepper
Sesame oil for brushing the burgers
4 sesame hamburger buns or 8–10 slider buns
Lime wedges for serving
Lettuce, sliced tomato, and other condiments for serving (optional)

1. Preparing the Ingredients.
2. Put the garlic, ginger, and one-third of the shrimp in a food processor; purée until smooth, stopping the machine to scrape down the sides as necessary. Add the remaining shrimp, basil, and shallots, season with salt and pepper, and pulse to chop. Form into 4 burgers about ¾ inch thick (or 8 to 10 sliders). Transfer to a plate, cover with plastic wrap, and chill until firm, at least 1 or up to 8 hours.
3. Turn the control knob to the high position, when the griddle is hot, brush the burgers on both sides with oil then put them on the griddle and cook until the bottoms brown and they come off easily, 5 to 7 minutes. Carefully turn and cook until opaque all the way through, 3 to 5 minutes. Put the buns, cut side down, on the griddle to toast. Serve the burgers on the toasted buns with lime wedges, as is, or dressed, however you like.

Nutrition: Calories: 444, Fat: 27 g, Carbs: 1 g, Protein: 47 g

Beet Burgers with Dates and Ginger

 Prep Time 10 min **Cook Time** 20 min **Servings** 2

1 pound beets, peeled and grated (about 5 cups)
1/2 cup packed pitted dates, broken into pieces
1/2 cup almonds
1 1-inch piece peeled fresh ginger, cut into coins
1/2 cup bulgur
Salt and pepper
¾ cup boiling red wine or water
1 tablespoon Dijon or other mustard
Cayenne or red chili flakes (optional)

1. Preparing the Ingredients
2. Put the beets in a food processor with the dates, almonds, and ginger; pulse until everything is well chopped but not quite a paste. Transfer the mixture to a large bowl and add the bulgur and a sprinkle of salt and pepper. Stir in the boiling wine, mustard, and cayenne to taste if you're using it, and cover the bowl with a plate. Let sit for 20 minutes for the bulgur to soften. Taste and adjust the seasonings. Shape into 12 burgers, put on a platter without touching, and refrigerate for at least 1 hour.
3. Turn the control knob to the high position, when the griddle is hot, place the burgers and cook for 10 minutes without flipping.
4. Serve with your preferred fixings or toppings.

Nutrition: Calories: 80, Fat: 5 g, Carbs: 3 g, Protein: 5 g

1 teaspoon salt
1 teaspoon black pepper
4 cloves garlic, chopped
4 hard rolls, split, or 8–10 slider buns

Nutrition: Calories: 444, Fat: 27 g, Carbs: 1 g, Protein: 47 g

Garlicky Pork Burgers

Prep Time 5 min   Cook Time 10 min   Servings 4

1. Preparing the Ingredients
2. Put the meat, salt, pepper, and garlic in a food processor and pulse until coarsely ground—finer than chopped, but not much. (If using pre-ground meat, put it in a bowl with the salt, pepper, and garlic and work them together gently with your hands.)
3. Handling the meat as little as possible to avoid compressing it, shape it lightly into 4 burgers, 1 to 11/2 inches thick. (You can do this several hours in advance; cover with plastic wrap and refrigerate until you're ready to cook)
4. Turn the control knob to the high position, when the griddle is hot, place the burgers on and cook for 10 minutes without flipping; the internal temperature should be 160°F (check with an instant-read thermometer, or nick with a small knife and peek inside).
5. Transfer to a platter. Toast the rolls. Serve the burgers on the rolls.

Cuban Pork Sandwich

 Prep Time 25 min Cook Time 180 min Servings 4

1 tablespoon butter
3 cups chicken stock
4 ciabatta bread
1/4 cup Dijon mustard
4 sliced dill pickle
1 lb. ham
1/4 cup mayonnaise
A rub of pulled pork
3 1/2 lbs. pork shoulder
8 oz. Swiss cheese, sliced
1 tablespoon vegetable oil
1 white onion, sliced

Nutrition: Calories: 80, Fat: 5 g, Carbs: 3 g, Protein: 5 g

1. Preheat the griddle to medium flame.
2. Season the pork shoulder generously using Pulled Pork Rub before placing it on the griddle pan. After 1 hour of cooking, flip the pork and continue to cook for another hour.
3. In an iron skillet, combine the onion and chicken stock. Cover the pork with a deep cast-iron skillet after transferring it to the skillet. Cook for two hours. After that, raise the temperature to 300° F and cook for another hour.
4. While the pork is still on the griddle, remove the cover and pull it with tongs. Because the stock will still have decreased, mix the pork in the decreased, seasoned stock with the onions.
5. Again, Pre-heat the griddle to a low heat setting.
6. On the griddle, melt the butter and oil, then toast the rolls by hand or with a metal spatula. Mix up the mustard and mayonnaise, then spread it on both sides of the rolls.
7. Place the pork, together with the cut ham, on the griddle in 4 parts. Cook for 2–3 minutes, turning the ham and pork halfway through. Pork, cheese, ham, and pickles are layered one on top of the other. Allow 1 minute for the cheese to melt. Return the rolls to a griddle, cut each filled portion in half, and stack two rolls on each prepared roll. Using the bottom of the metal spatula, press each sandwich down. Flip carefully and press down once more.
8. Remove the sandwiches off the griddle and keep them warm until ready to serve.

Jalapeño Stuffed Burger

 Prep Time 15 min   **Cook Time** 35 min   **Servings** 1

1. Preparing the Ingredients.
2. Combine ground beef, sea salt, pepper, cilantro, onion, and jalapeño. Divide the ground beef mixture into 4 balls. Stuff each ball with a chunk of Cheddar. Rub burgers with olive oil.
3. Grill for about 5 minutes per side or to desired doneness. Top burgers with sliced Cheddar.
4. Spread each roll with margarine. Grill to the desired degree of doneness. Serve burgers topped with pickled jalapeños. 4 1/2 oz. Cheddar cheese, cut into chunks 2 tablespoons of olive oil, 4 slices of Cheddar cheese, 4 brioche rolls 1/4 cup margarine, and 16 pickled jalapeño rings. If you have fresh sliced jalapeños, heat 1 cup vinegar, and 1/4 cup sugar, then pour over the peppers and let sit for 30 Minutes for a quick pickle.

Burger Mixture
2 lb. ground beef
1 teaspoon sea salt
1 teaspoon ground black pepper
3 tablespoons cilantro, chopped 1/2 small onion, peeled and minced
1 jalapeño, seeded and chopped

Nutrition: Calories: 902, Fat: 74 g, Carbs: 60 g, Protein: 65 g

Pineapple Teriyaki Turkey Burgers

 Prep Time 5 min   **Cook Time** 15 min   **Servings** 4

1 teaspoon BBQ rub
1 can of sliced pineapple
4 slices of Swiss cheese
1 cup fresh raw spinach, stems removed
4 sets of hamburger buns
Patty
1 lb. ground turkey
1/2 cup breadcrumbs
1/4 cup teriyaki sauce
1 small yellow onion, diced
2 tablespoons finely chopped parsley
2 cloves garlic, minced
1 egg, beaten

1. Preparing the Ingredients.
2. In a large mixing bowl, combine all patty ingredients and mix thoroughly by hand.
3. Divide the mixture into four equal parts. Form the four portions into patties and lay them on parchment paper. Sprinkle each patty evenly with BBQ rub. Place in refrigerator for 30 Minutes.
4. Bring the griddle to high heat. When the griddle is hot, place the burgers and pineapple slices. Cook for 4 minutes without flipping. Remove the burgers and cover to keep warm.
5. After burgers are flipped over, add a slice of Swiss cheese to each patty and allow to melt as the patty finishes cooking. Remove from griddle.
6. Layer burgers on buns with spinach and pineapple.

Nutrition: Calories: 167, Carbs: 43 g, Fat: 3.4 g, Protein: 1 g

Thick Stacked Sizzling Burgers on The Griddle

Prep Time 15 min   **Cook Time** 5 min   **Servings** 6

1-1/2 pounds ground beef, 80% to 85% lean
6 hamburger buns
1/4 stick butter (use oil as a substitute if desired)
Pinch salt
Pinch fresh black pepper
6 slices cheese
Burger toppings:
2 sliced tomatoes,
1/4 onion (sliced)
2 pickles
3 tablespoons Ketchup
2 tablespoons Mustard
6 lettuce leaves

1. Preheat the griddle to sear with the unit closed.
2. Shape ground beef into 6 big and chunky patties, then melt butter on the griddle over medium heat. Lightly butter the buns, then toast them to your desired liking. Move the buns to a clean plate. Then, using the same pan, cook the patties for several minutes. Add a pinch of salt and pepper to each and continue to cook for 3 to 4 min.
3. Flip the burgers and repeat the process, adding a little more salt and pepper than before. Cook for another several minutes or until cooked to your desired liking

Nutrition: Calories: 980, Fats 43 g, Carbs: 13 g, Protein: 9 g

1. Preheat the griddle to high heat.
2. Spray griddle top with cooking spray.
3. Add all ingredients into the mixing bowl and mix until well combined.
4. Make small patties from mixture and place on hot griddle top and cook until golden brown from both sides.
5. Serve and enjoy.

Yummy Turkey Burger

Prep Time 5 min   **Cook Time** 5 min   **Servings** 8

1 lb. ground turkey
1 egg, lightly beaten
1 cup Monterey jack cheese, grated
1 cup carrot, grated
1 cup cauliflower, grated
2 garlic cloves, minced
1/2 cup onion, minced
3/4 cup breadcrumbs
Pepper
Salt

Nutrition: Calories: 299, Fat: 15 g, Carbs: 14 g, Protein: 3 g

Big Burger

Prep Time 20 min   **Cook Time** 10 min   **Servings** 4

11/4 pounds lean ground beef
1/2 teaspoon salt
1/2 teaspoon freshly ground black pepper
Seasoning of your choice (such as a dash of Worcestershire or hot sauce, or 1 teaspoon Spicy Spanish Rub
4 slices cheese such as American, Cheddar, or Swiss (about 4 ounces), or 1/4 cup crumbled blue or goat cheese
4 toasted buns
4 beefsteak tomato slices
4 leaves of romaine lettuce

1. Preparing the Ingredients.
2. Bring the griddle to medium-high heat.
3. Put the beef in a medium bowl and add the salt, pepper, and your preferred seasonings. Using a fork, mix the seasonings into the meat and then, with your hands, form the mixture into 4 patties, each about 1 inch thick.
4. When the griddle is hot, place the burgers on the griddle and cook for 4 minutes without flipping. Cooking is complete when the internal temperature of the beef reaches at least 145°F on a food thermometer. If needed, cook for up to 5 more minutes.
5. Lay the cheese over the burgers and cook for 30 seconds, just until the cheese melts.
6. Set the burgers onto the bottom halves of the buns, add a slice of tomato and a leaf of lettuce to each burger, and cover with the tops of the buns. Serve immediately.

Nutrition: Calories: 178, Fat: 1 g, Carbs: 47 g, Protein: 2 g

Vegetable and Side Dishes

6 whole artichokes
1/2-gallon water
3 tablespoons Sea salt
Olive oil
Sea salt to taste
1/4 cup raw honey
1/4 cup boiling water
3 tablespoons Dijon mustard

Griddled Artichokes with Honey Dijon

 Prep Time 15 min **Cook Time** 15 min **Servings** 4

1. Cut the artichokes in half lengthwise, top to bottom.
2. Mix the 3 tablespoons of sea salt and water. Place the artichokes in the brine for 30 minutes to several hours before cooking.
3. Heat the griddle to medium.
4. Remove the artichokes from the brine, drizzle with olive oil on the cut side, and season with sea salt.
5. Grill for 15 minutes on each side and cut the side down first.
6. Turn the griddle down to low, and turn the artichokes cut-side down while you mix the honey, boiling water, and Dijon.
7. Turn the artichokes back over, and brush the Dijon mix well over the cut side until it is all absorbed.
8. Serve alongside a Protein: like salmon, beef, pork, or chicken, or with rice or potatoes for a vegetarian option.

Nutrition: Calories: 601, Fat: 57 g, Protein: 8 g, Carbs: 21 g

Stir Fry Mushrooms

 Prep Time 15 min **Cook Time** 15 min **Servings** 3

1. Preheat the griddle to high heat.
2. Add 2 tablespoons of oil to the hot griddle top.
3. Add mushrooms, garlic, thyme, pepper, and salt, and sauté mushrooms until tender.
4. Drizzle the remaining oil and serve.

10 oz mushrooms, sliced
1/4 cup olive oil
1 tablespoon garlic, minced
1/4 teaspoon dried thyme
Pepper
Salt

Nutrition: Calories: 253, Fat: 25 g, Carbs: 6 g, Protein: 4 g

Roasted Tomatoes with Hot Pepper Sauce

 Prep Time 15 min   **Cook Time** 1-1/2 hour   **Servings** 3

2 lbs. tomatoes; Roma fresh
1 lb. spaghetti
2 tablespoons chopped garlic
1/2 cup olive oil
3 tablespoons chopped parsley
Salt, hot pepper, and black pepper, to taste

1. Set the griddle to preheat and push the temperature to 400°F.
2. Now take the tomatoes, wash them thoroughly, and cut them into halves, lengthwise.
3. Place it on a baking dish while making sure that the cut side faces upwards
4. Sprinkle it with chopped parsley, salt, black pepper, and garlic.
5. Also, put 1/4 cup of olive oil over them
6. Now place it on the griddle for 1-1/2 hour
7. The tomatoes will shrink, and the skin is likely to get slightly blackened
8. Now remove the tomatoes from the baking dish and place them in the food processor and puree it well
9. Drop the pasta into the boiling salt water and cook it until it turns tender
10. Drain and toss it immediately with the pureed tomatoes mix
11. Now add the leftover 1/4 cup of raw olive oil along with crumbled hot pepper as per taste
12. Toss well and serve.

Nutrition: Calories: 45, Fat: 1 g, Carbs: 8 g, Protein: 2 g

Italian Zucchini Slices

 Prep Time 15 min   **Cook Time** 5 min   **Servings** 3

2 zucchini, cut into 1/2-inch thick slices
1 teaspoon Italian seasoning
2 garlic cloves, minced
1/4 cup butter, melted
1 1/2 tablespoons fresh parsley, chopped
1 tablespoon fresh lemon juice
Pepper
Salt

1. In a small bowl, mix melted butter, lemon juice, Italian seasoning, garlic, pepper, and salt.
2. Brush zucchini slices with melted butter mixture.
3. Preheat the griddle to high heat.
4. Place zucchini slices on the griddle top and cook for 2 minutes per side.
5. Transfer zucchini slices to a serving plate and garnish with parsley.
6. Serve and enjoy.

Nutrition: Calories: 125, Fat: 12 g, Carbs: 4 g, Protein: 2 g

---

Roasted Asparagus

 Prep Time 15 min   **Cook Time** 7 min   **Servings** 2

1 pound medium to thin asparagus, woody stems snapped off and discarded
2 tablespoons olive oil
1/4 teaspoon salt
1/2 teaspoon freshly ground black pepper
1/4 cup grated Parmesan cheese, preferably freshly grated

1. Preparing the Ingredients
2. Toss the asparagus with olive oil, salt, and pepper in a medium bowl.
3. Bring the griddle to medium-high heat. Oil the griddle and allow it to heat until the oil is shimmering but not smoking. Grill the asparagus spears for about 7 minutes until they are tender.
4. Serve hot or at room temperature, sprinkled with Parmesan.

Nutrition: Calories: 102, Fat: 9 g, Protein: 4 g

Griddled Zucchini Squash Spears

Prep Time 5 min **Cook Time** 5 min **Servings** 2

4 midsized zucchini
2 springs thyme with the leaves pulled out
1 tablespoon sherry vinegar
2 tablespoons olive oil
Salt and pepper as per your taste

1. Take the zucchini and cut off the ends
2. Now cut each of them in half and then cut every half into thirds
3. Take all the leftover ingredients in a midsized zip lock bag and then add spears to it
4. Toss it and mix well so that it coats the zucchini
5. Start to preheat the griddle to medium-high
6. Remove the spears from the bag and place them directly on the griddle grate. Make sure that the side faces downwards
7. Cook for 3 to 4 minutes per side until you can see the griddle starts popping up, and the zucchini should become tender too
8. Remove from the griddle and add more thyme leaves if needed
9. Serve and enjoy.

Nutrition: Calories: 235, Carbs: 21 g, Fat: 16 g, Protein: 8 g

---

Griddled Eggplant with Feta and Lemon

Prep Time 15 min **Cook Time** 25 min **Servings** 3

1 large eggplant, cut into 1/2-inch slices
1 tablespoon salt
3 tablespoons olive oil
4 ounces feta cheese, crumbled
1/2 teaspoon sweet paprika
Freshly ground black pepper
1 lemon, cut in half

1. Preparing the Ingredients
2. Spread the eggplant slices on a rimmed baking sheet and sprinkle with half of the salt. Flip the slices and sprinkle with the remaining salt. Let sit for 15 minutes to take away some of the bitterness of the eggplant. Transfer the slices to sheets of paper towels and pat dry.
3. Bring the griddle to medium-high heat. Oil the griddle and allow it to heat until the oil is shimmering but not smoking. Brush both sides of the eggplant slices with olive oil. Grill for about 6 minutes, until the slices are golden brown.
4. Transfer the eggplant to a serving platter and top with the feta, paprika, some pepper, and a squirt of lemon juice. Serve hot or at room temperature.

Nutrition: Calories: 204, Fat: 17 g, Carbs: 0 g, Protein: 6 g

---

Griddled Sweet Potatoes

Prep Time 15 min **Cook Time** 7 min **Servings** 1

1 cup sweet potatoes
Olive oil
Sea salt to taste

1. Slice the sweet potatoes in half lengthwise.
2. Brush the entire sweet potato with olive oil and season liberally with sea salt.
3. Heat the griddle to high, and grill the sweet potatoes cut-side down for 5–7 minutes. Turn them over and grill on medium heat until the sweet potatoes are tender.
4. Let the potatoes relax for several minutes before serving.

Nutrition: Calories: 160, Fat: 11 g, Carbs: 6 g, Protein: 1 g

Griddled Eggplant Napoleon

 Prep Time 15 min   **Cook Time** 15 minutes   **Servings** 1

1 Eggplant sliced lengthwise into half-inch slices
Olive Oil brushed
Salt to taste
1 cup Heirloom Tomatoes sliced thin
1 tbs Lemon squeezed
1 tbs Balsamic Vinegar drizzled
Fresh Basil garnished
8 Haloumi cheese sliced to 1/4 inch thick and griddled

1. Slice the eggplant thin lengthwise and brush with the olive oil and season with the sea salt.
2. Slice the Halloumi to 1/4 inch and grill on high for one minute per side
3. Turn the griddle on high and cook the eggplant for several minutes per side until the griddle marks are prevalent.
4. Layer the eggplant with griddled halloumi and sliced tomatoes. Squeeze the lemon juice over the top, drizzle the balsamic vinegar, and garnish with slightly torn fresh basil.

Nutrition: Calories: 232, Fat: 7 g, Carbs: 9 g, Protein: 11 g

Stir Fry Cabbage

 Prep Time 5 min   **Cook Time** 5 min   **Servings** 3

1 cabbage head, tear cabbage leaves, washed and drained
2 green onions, sliced
1 tablespoon ginger, minced
2 garlic cloves, minced
1 tablespoon soy sauce
1/2 tablespoons vinegar
4 dried chilies
2 tablespoons olive oil
1/2 teaspoons salt

1. Preheat the griddle to high heat.
2. Add oil to the hot griddle top.
3. Add ginger, garlic, and green onion and sauté for 2-3 minutes.
4. Add dried chilies and sauté for 30 seconds.
5. Add cabbage, vinegar, soy sauce, and salt and stir fry for 1-2 minutes over high heat until cabbage wilted.
6. Serve and enjoy.

Nutrition: Calories: 115, Fat: 7 g, Carbs: 12 g, Protein: 3 g

Zucchini Antipasto

1/4 cup olive oil
3 garlic cloves, minced
1 tablespoon fresh thyme leaves or 1/2 teaspoon dried thyme
1/4 teaspoon salt
1/4 teaspoon freshly ground black pepper
4 medium zucchini, cut lengthwise into 1/4-inch-thick slices
1 tablespoon balsamic vinegar

 Prep Time 10 min   **Cook Time** 6 min   **Servings** 2

1. Preparing the Ingredients
2. Whisk together the olive oil, garlic, thyme, salt, and pepper in a large bowl.
3. Add the zucchini and toss to coat.
4. Bring the griddle to medium-high heat. Oil the griddle and allow it to heat until the oil is shimmering but not smoking.
5. Grill for about 6 minutes until the zucchini slices are very tender.
6. Serve either hot off the griddle or at room temperature, sprinkled with vinegar.

Nutrition: Calories: 102, Fat: 9 g, Protein: 4 g

Healthy Zucchini Noodles

 Prep Time 5 min   **Cook Time** 7 min   **Servings** 2

1. Preheat the griddle to high heat.
2. Add oil to the hot griddle top.
3. Add onion and sauté for 4-5 minutes.
4. Add zucchini noodles and cook for 2 minutes.
5. Add sesame seeds, teriyaki sauce, and soy sauce, and cook for 4-5 minutes.
6. Serve and enjoy.

4 small zucchini, spiralized
1 tablespoon soy sauce
2 onions, spiralized
2 tablespoons olive oil
1 tablespoon sesame seeds
2 tablespoons teriyaki sauce

Nutrition: Calories: 124, Fat: 8 g, Carbs: 11 g, Protein: 3 g

Griddled Spicy Sweet Potatoes

 Prep Time 10 min   **Cook Time** 30 min   **Servings** 1

2 lb. sweet potatoes, cut into chunks
1 red onion, chopped
2 tablespoons oil
2 tablespoons orange juice
1 tablespoon roasted cinnamon
1 tablespoon salt
1/4 tablespoon Chipotle chili pepper

1. Preheat the griddle to 425°F with the lid closed.
2. Toss the sweet potatoes with onion, oil, and juice.
3. In a mixing bowl, mix cinnamon, salt, and pepper, then sprinkle the mixture over the sweet potatoes.
4. Spread the potatoes on a lined baking dish in a single layer.
5. Place the baking dish on the griddle and cook for 30 minutes or until the sweet potatoes are tender.
6. Serve and enjoy.

Nutrition: Calories: 145, Fat: 5 g, Carbs: 19 g, Protein: 2 g

Stir Fry Bok Choy

 Prep Time 5 min    **Cook Time** 4 min   **Servings** 1

2 heads Bok choy, trimmed and cut crosswise
1 teaspoon sesame oil
2 teaspoons soy sauce
2 tablespoons water
1 tablespoon butter
1 tablespoon peanut oil
1 tablespoon oyster sauce
1/2 teaspoons salt

1. In a small bowl, mix soy sauce, oyster sauce, sesame oil, and water and set aside.
2. Preheat the griddle to high heat.
3. Add oil to the hot griddle top.
4. Add Bok choy and salt and stir fry for 2 minutes.
5. Add butter and soy sauce mixture and stir fry for 1-2 minutes.
6. Serve and enjoy.

Nutrition: Calories: 145, Fat: 5 g, Carbs: 19 g, Protein: 2 g

Wilted Spinach

 Prep Time 15 min **Cook Time** 5 min **Servings** 1

1. Preparing the Ingredients
2. In a medium bowl, toss the spinach with olive oil, garlic powder, and salt.
3. Bring the griddle to medium-high heat. Oil the griddle and allow it to heat until the oil is shimmering but not smoking. Spread the spinach in an even layer over the griddle and cook for 30 seconds. The leaves should wilt but retain just a bit of crunch. Transfer to a serving bowl and squeeze a bit of lemon juice on top. Serve immediately.

8 ounces fresh baby spinach
1 tablespoon olive oil
1/4 teaspoon garlic powder
1/4 teaspoon salt
1 lemon, halved

Nutrition: Calories: 44, Fat: 4 g, Carbs: 32 g, Protein: 2 g

Griddled Yellow Potatoes

 Prep Time 15 min **Cook Time** 15 min   **Servings** 1

1 cup yellow potatoes
1 tbs Olive oil
Sea salt and black pepper to taste
Paprika

1. Slice the potatoes in half lengthwise, and place them into a large bag or bowl.
2. Drizzle them with olive oil, and stir or shake to coat the potatoes.
3. Add the salt, pepper, and paprika to taste, and stir or shake until completely combined.
4. Preheat the griddle to medium, and spray it with oil.
5. Place the potatoes sliced-side down, and griddle for several minutes or until you can feel tender on the cut side.
6. Turn the potatoes over and cook until they are tender through.
7. Remove from heat and serve.

Nutrition: Calories: 280, Fat: 11 g, Carbs: 8 g, Protein: 4 g

---

Griddled Asparagus and Honey Glazed Carrots

 Prep Time 15 min **Cook Time** 50 min   **Servings** 2

1 bunch asparagus, trimmed ends
1 lb. carrots, peeled
2 tablespoons olive oil
Sea salt to taste
2 tablespoons honey
Lemon zest

1. Sprinkle the asparagus with oil and sea salt. Drizzle the carrots with honey and salt.
2. Preheat the to 165°F with the lid closed for 15 minutes.
3. Place the carrots in the and cook for 15 minutes. Add asparagus and cook for 20 more minutes or until cooked through.
4. Top the carrots and asparagus with lemon zest. Enjoy.

Nutrition: Calories: 189, Fat: 30 g, Carbs: 10 g, Protein: 4 g

Stir Fry Vegetables

 Prep Time 5 min   **Cook Time** 5 min   **Servings** 1

1. Preheat the griddle to high heat.
2. In a large bowl, toss vegetables with olive oil.
3. Transfer vegetables onto the hot griddle top and stir fry until vegetables are tender.
4. Serve and enjoy.

2 medium potatoes, cut into small pieces
3 medium carrots, peeled and cut into small pieces
1/4 cup olive oil
1 small rutabaga, peeled and cut into small pieces
2 medium parsnips, peeled and cut into small pieces
Pepper
Salt

Nutrition: Calories: 218,Fat: 12.8 g,Carbs: 25.2,Sugar 6.2 g, Protein: 2.8 g, Cholesterol: 0 mg

Easy Seared Green Beans

 Prep Time 15 min   **Cook Time** 7 min   **Servings** 1

1 1/2 lbs. green beans, trimmed
1 1/2 tablespoons rice vinegar
3 tablespoons soy sauce
1 1/2 tablespoons sesame oil
2 tablespoons sesame seeds, toasted
1 1/2 tablespoons brown sugar
1/4 teaspoons black pepper

1. Cook green beans in boiling water for 3 minutes and drain well.
2. Transfer green beans to chilled ice water and drain again. Pat dry green beans.
3. Preheat the griddle to high heat.
4. Add oil to the hot griddle top.
5. Add green beans and stir fry for 2 minutes.
6. Add soy sauce, brown sugar, vinegar, and pepper and stir fry for 2 minutes more.
7. Add sesame seeds and toss well to coat.
8. Serve and enjoy.

Nutrition: Calories: 100, Fat: 5 g, Carbs: 12 g, Protein: 3 g

Griddled Mexican Street Corn

6 ears of corn on the cob
1 tablespoon olive oil
Kosher salt and pepper to taste
1/4 cup mayo
1/4 cup sour cream
1 tablespoon garlic paste
1/2 tablespoons chili powder
Pinch of ground red pepper
1/2 cup coria cheese, crumbled
1/4 cup cilantro, chopped
6 lime wedges

 Prep Time 10 min   **Cook Time** 25 min   **Servings** 3

1. Brush the corn with oil.
2. Sprinkle with salt.
3. Place the corn on the griddle set at 350°F. Cook for 25 minutes as you turn it occasionally.
4. Meanwhile, mix mayo, cream, garlic, chili, and red pepper until well combined.
5. Let it rest for some minutes, then brush with the mayo mixture.
6. Sprinkle cottage cheese, more chili powder, and cilantro. Serve with lime wedges. Enjoy.

Nutrition: Calories: 144, Fat: 5 g, Carbs: 10 g, Protein: 5 g

Griddled Eggplant

1 eggplant (large)
4 tablespoons coconut aminos
2 tablespoons avocado oil
2 teaspoons cumin (ground)
2 teaspoons smoked paprika
2 teaspoons coriander (ground)
2 teaspoons cumin (ground)
1/2 teaspoon cayenne pepper
1/2 teaspoon garlic powder
1/2 teaspoon sea salt

 Prep Time 5 min   **Cook Time** 3 min   **Servings** 2

1. Cut the eggplant lengthwise into 1/4-inch slices. Drizzle and brush the eggplant slices with Coconut Aminos and avocado oil.
2. In a small mixing bowl, combine the spices. Sprinkle the mix on the slices on both sides, ensuring they are fully coated.
3. Preheat your griddle to medium-high heat and place the slices. Griddle each side for 3 minutes till they become tender.
4. Remove from the griddle and enjoy.

Nutrition: Calories: 62, Fat: 2 g, Carbs: 11 g, Protein: 2 g

Griddled Asparagus and Honey Glazed Carrots

 Prep Time 5 min   **Cook Time** 50 min   **Servings** 1

1 lb. carrots, peeled
2 tablespoons olive oil
Sea salt to taste
2 tablespoons honey
Lemon zest

1. Sprinkle the asparagus with oil and sea salt. Drizzle the carrots with honey and salt.
2. Preheat the to 165°F with the lid closed for 15 minutes.
3. Place the carrots in the and cook for 15 minutes. Add asparagus and cook for 20 more minutes or until cooked through.
4. Top the carrots and asparagus with lemon zest. Enjoy.

Nutrition: Calories: 1680, Fat: 30 g, Carbs: 10 g, Protein: 4 g

Griddled Zucchini Squash Spears

 Prep Time 10 min   **Cook Time** 20 min   **Servings** 1

4 zucchinis, cleaned and ends cut
2 tablespoons olive oil
1 tablespoon sherry vinegar
2 thyme leaves pulled
Salt and pepper to taste

1. Cut the zucchini into halves, then cut each half thirds.
2. Add the rest of the ingredients to a zip lock bag with the zucchini pieces. Toss to mix well.
3. Preheat the temperature to 350°F with the lid closed for 15 minutes.
4. Remove the zucchini from the bag and place them on the griddle grate with the cut side down.
5. Cook for 4 minutes until the zucchini are tender
6. Remove from griddle and serve with thyme leaves. Enjoy.

Nutrition: Calories: 74, Fat: 5 g, Carbs: 6 g, Protein: 3 g

Griddled Lemon Pepper Chicken Salad

 Prep Time 5 min   **Cook Time** 15 min   **Servings** 1

1 Lemon Pepper Chicken Breast
1 head Romaine Lettuce
1 Crouton
1 cup Parmesan Cheese
2 Balsamic Vinaigrette Dressing

1. Using the flat side of a meat mallet, pound the chicken breast flat until it is a uniform thickness of about ¾ thick. This will help the chicken cook more evenly, taste better and slice more easily!
2. Preheat your griddle to medium-high heat and cook for about 10 minutes per side, flipping only once, until the chicken reaches 165°F internal temperature.
3. Remove the chicken from the griddle and let sit for 5 minutes. Slice into strips.
4. Place the lemon pepper chicken strips on top of a bed of lettuce and add croutons, cheese, and dressing to your taste. Other suggested toppings include cherry tomatoes and fresh cucumber slices!

Nutrition: Calories: 214, Fat: 8 g, Carbs: 5 g, Protein: 28 g

Baba Ghanoush

2 medium-large eggplants (about 2 pounds total), with stems on
1/3 cup tahini
1/4 cup fresh lemon juice
2 large cloves of garlic, or to taste, minced
Salt and pepper
4 pita bread for serving
Good-quality olive oil for drizzling
1/4 cup chopped fresh parsley for garnish

 Prep Time 15 min   **Cook Time** 31 min   **Servings** 4

1. Preparing the Ingredients
2. Pierce the eggplants in several places with a thin knife or skewer.
3. Bring the griddle to high heat. Oil the griddle. Put them on the griddle. Cook until the eggplants are blackened on all sides and collapsed for 25 to 30 Minutes. Transfer to a bowl.
4. Whisk the tahini and lemon juice in a small bowl until smooth. Stir in the garlic and sprinkle with salt and pepper.
5. When the eggplants are cool enough to handle, peel off and discard the burnt skin. Mash the flesh with a fork. Beat in the tahini mixture until the dip is smooth. Taste and adjust the seasoning. (You can make the dip up to 3 days in advance; cover and refrigerate.)
6. Toast the pita directly over the griddle, turning once, until they're warm, 1 to 2 minutes per side. Cut into wedges. Transfer the baba ghanoush to a shallow serving bowl, drizzle the top with olive oil, sprinkle with the parsley, and serve with warm pita wedges.

Nutrition: Calories: 145, Fat: 5 g, Carbs: 19 g, Protein: 2 g

Stuffed Eggplant with Ginger, Sesame, And Soy

 Prep Time 15 min   **Cook Time** 30 min   **Servings** 1

2 small eggplants (about 8 ounces each)
1/4 cup minced fresh cilantro
2 tablespoons soy sauce
1 tablespoon minced fresh ginger
1 teaspoon sesame oil
Lime wedges for serving

1. Preparing the Ingredients
2. Cut the eggplants in half lengthwise for long eggplant or through the equator for globe eggplant. Mix the cilantro, soy sauce, ginger, and oil well in a small bowl. Work the flavor paste over the cut surfaces of the eggplants, pushing it into the slits.
3. Bring the griddle to medium-high heat. Oil the griddle and allow it to heat until the oil is shimmering but not smoking. Put the eggplant halves on the griddle and cook until the skin has crisped, the tops are browned, and the flesh is fork-tender, 25 to 30 minutes; rotate and turn about halfway through for even cooking. Transfer to a platter and serve hot, warm, or at room temperature with lime wedges.

Nutrition: Calories: 435, Fat: 32 g, Carbs: 18 g, Protein: 21 g

Griddled Corn with Soy Butter and Sesame

 Prep Time 10 min   **Cook Time** 12 min   **Servings** 2

3 tablespoons unsalted butter
1 scallion, both white and green parts, finely chopped
2 tablespoons soy sauce
4 ears of sweet corn, shucked and cut or broken in half crosswise
1 tablespoon toasted sesame seeds

1. Preparing the Ingredients
2. Melt the butter in a saucepan over medium heat. Add the scallion and cook until it loses its rawness, about 1 minute (you don't want the scallion to be brown). Stir in the soy sauce and remove the saucepan from the heat.
3. Bring the griddle to medium-high heat. Oil the griddle and allow it to heat until the oil is shimmering but not smoking.
4. Arrange the ears of corn on the griddle. The corn will be done after cooking for 2 to 3 minutes per side (8 to 12 minutes in all) until nicely browned on all sides, basting it with a little of the soy butter. Use a light touch as you baste; you don't want to drip a lot of butter into the griddle.
5. Transfer the corn to a platter. Brush it with any remaining soy butter, sprinkle the sesame seeds over it, and serve at once.
6. To toast sesame seeds, place them in a dry cast-iron or another heavy skillet (don't use a nonstick skillet for this). Cook the sesame seeds over medium heat until lightly browned, about 3 minutes, shaking the skillet to ensure that they toast evenly. Transfer the toasted sesame seeds to a heatproof bowl to cool.

Nutrition: Calories: 44, Fat: 4 g, Carbs: 8 g, Protein: 2 g

Fennel-orange Slaw with Rosemary and Pickled Red Onion

Prep Time 5 min **Cook Time** 10 min **Servings** 2

1/2 cup rice vinegar
1/4 cup sugar
1 small red onion, halved, thinly sliced, and pulled apart
2 pounds fennel
2 tablespoons good-quality olive oil, plus more for brushing
3 navel oranges
1 teaspoon minced fresh rosemary
Salt and pepper

Nutrition: Calories: 280, Fat: 11 g, Carbs: 8 g, Protein: 4 g

1. Preparing the Ingredients
2. Put the vinegar and sugar in a small nonreactive saucepan and bring to a boil. Remove from the heat, add the onion, and stir to combine. Let it rest while you prepare the fire. Or you can do this earlier in the day, cover, and let sit at room temperature.
3. Trim the fennel bulbs, reserving the feathery fronds. Cut the fennel in half from the stalk end to the base; brush with some oil. Cut the peel from the oranges with a small knife, deep enough to remove the white pith. Slice the oranges across into 1/4-inch rounds, then cut the rounds into wedges. Put in a large bowl.
4. Bring the griddle to medium-high heat. Oil the griddle and allow it to heat until the oil is shimmering but not smoking. Put the fennel on the griddle and cook until the fennel is crisp-tender and browned or charred in spots, 8 to 10 Minutes. Transfer to a cutting board and thinly slice across into crescents. Add to the oranges. Use a slotted spoon to transfer the onion to the bowl; reserve the brine. Mince enough fennel fronds to make 2 tablespoons
5. Add the oil, 1 tablespoon of the brine, the rosemary, the minced fronds, and some salt and pepper. Toss to coat, taste and adjust the seasoning, and serve. Or prepare the slaw up to a day ahead, cover, and refrigerate.

Crisp Baby Artichokes with Lemon Aioli

 Prep Time 15 min **Cook Time** 10 min **Servings** 4

2 tablespoons good-quality olive oil
Grated zest and juice of 1 lemon
8 baby artichokes
1/2 cup mayonnaise
1 teaspoon minced garlic, or more to taste
Salt and pepper

Nutrition: Calories: 122, Fat: 8 g, Carbs: 9 g, Protein: 6 g

1. Preparing the Ingredients
2. Whisk the oil and lemon juice in a large bowl. Peel away and discard the outer layers of each artichoke until the leaves are half yellow and half green. With a sharp knife, cut across the top of the artichoke to remove the green tops. Leave 1 inch of stem and use a paring knife or vegetable peeler to trim the bottom, so no green remains. Cut the artichoke in half lengthwise from top to bottom. As each artichoke is trimmed, add it to the olive oil mixture and toss it to coat evenly; this helps delay discoloring. (You can cover the bowl and refrigerate for up to several hours.)
3. Make the aioli: Put the mayonnaise, garlic, and lemon zest in a small bowl, sprinkle with salt and pepper and whisk to combine. Taste and adjust the seasoning.
4. Bring the griddle to medium-high heat. Oil the griddle and allow it to heat until the oil is shimmering but not smoking. Put the artichokes cut side down on the griddle and cook until tender and charred, 8 to 10 Minutes. Transfer to a plate and serve with the aioli for dipping.

Tomato Melts with Spinach Salad

 Prep Time 5 min   **Cook Time** 10 min   **Servings** 4

1 or 2 large fresh tomatoes (enough for 4 thick slices across)
2 tablespoons good-quality olive oil, plus more for brushing
Salt and pepper
2 teaspoons white wine vinegar
1 teaspoon Dijon mustard
3 cups baby spinach
6 slices of Cheddar cheese (about 4 ounces)

1. Preparing the Ingredients
2. Core the tomatoes and cut 4 thick slices (about 1 inch); save the trimmings. Brush them with oil and sprinkle with salt and pepper on both sides. Whisk the 2 tablespoons of oil, vinegar, and mustard together in a bowl. Chop the trimmings from the tomatoes; add them to the dressing along with the spinach, and toss until evenly coated.
3. Bring the griddle to medium-high heat. Oil the griddle and allow it to heat until the oil is shimmering but not smoking. Put the tomato slices and cook for 3 Minutes. Turn the tomatoes and top each slice with a slice of Cheddar, and cook until the cheese is melted for 2 to 3 minutes. Transfer to plates and serve with the salad on top.

Nutrition: Calories: 218, Fat: 13 g, Carbs: 25 g, Protein: 3 g

Cauliflower With Garlic and Anchovies

 Prep Time 5 min   **Cook Time** 20 min   **Servings** 3

1 head cauliflower (11/2–2 pounds)
6 tablespoons good-quality olive oil
6 oil-packed anchovy fillets, chopped, or more to taste
1 tablespoon minced garlic
1/2 teaspoon red chili flakes, or to taste
Optional:
Salt and pepper (optional)
Chopped fresh parsley for garnish

1. Preparing the Ingredients
2. Break or cut the cauliflower into florets about 11/2 inches across; put in a bowl.
3. Put the oil, anchovies, garlic, and red pepper if using it in a small skillet over medium-low heat. Cook, stirring occasionally until the anchovies begin to break up and the garlic just begins to color for about 5 minutes. Taste and add more anchovies or some salt and pepper. Pour half of the oil mixture over the cauliflower; toss to coat evenly with it. Bring the griddle to medium-high heat. Oil the griddle and allow it to heat until the oil is shimmering but not smoking. Put the florets in a single and cook until the cauliflower is as tender and browned as you like it, 5 Minutes for crisp-tender to 10 minutes for fully tender. Transfer to a serving bowl, drizzle over the remaining sauce and the parsley, toss gently and serve warm or at room temperature.

Nutrition: Calories: 100, Fat: 5 g, Carbs: 11 g, Protein: 3 g

Beets And Greens with Lemon-dill Vinaigrette

 Prep Time 20 min **Cook Time** 45 min **Servings** 2

1. Preparing the Ingredients
2. Cut the greens off the beets. Throw away any wilted or discolored leaves; rinse the remainder well to remove any grit and drain. Trim the root ends of the beets and scrub well under running water. Pat the leaves and beets dry. Toss the beets with 2 tablespoons of the oil and a sprinkle of salt until evenly coated.
3. Bring the griddle to medium-high heat. Oil the griddle and allow it to heat until the oil is shimmering but not smoking. Put the beets on the griddle, and cook until a knife inserted in the center goes through with no resistance, 35 to 40 minutes total. Transfer to a plate and let sit until cool enough to handle.
4. Toss the beet greens in the reserved bowl to coat in oil. Put the greens on the griddle and cook until they're bright green and browned in spots, 2 to 5 minutes total. Keep a close eye on them; if they're on too long, they'll crisp up to the point where they'll shatter. Transfer to a plate.
5. Put the remaining 1/2 cup oil and the lemon juice in a serving bowl and whisk until thickened. Stir in the dill and some salt and pepper. Peel the skin from the beets and cut it into halves or quarters. Cut the stems from the leaves in 1-inch lengths; cut the leaves across into ribbons. Put the beets, leaves, and stems in the bowl and toss with the vinaigrette until coated. Serve warm or at room temperature. Or makeup to several hours ahead, cover, and refrigerate to serve chilled.

11/2 pounds small beets, with fresh-looking greens still attached if possible
1/2 cup plus 2 tablespoons good-quality olive oil
Salt and pepper
3 tablespoons fresh lemon juice
4 tablespoons minced fresh dill

Nutrition: Calories: 160, Fat: 7 g, Carbs: 20 g, Protein: 5 g

---

Griddled Tempeh

 Prep Time 5 min **Cook Time** 60 min **Servings** 2

1. Preparing the Ingredients
2. Brush the tempeh with oil and sprinkle with salt on both sides.
3. Bring the griddle to high heat. Oil the griddle Put the tempeh and cook until it develops a crust and releases easily from the grates, about 6. Sprinkle with more salt and some pepper if you like, and serve.

1 8-ounce piece of tempeh
Good-quality olive oil for brushing
Salt
Pepper (optional)

Nutrition: Calories: 386, Fat: 19 g, Carbs: 49 g, Protein: 7 g

Griddled Polenta

 Prep Time 10 min   **Cook Time** 10 min   **Servings** 2

2 tablespoons butter, plus more for the pan
1/2 cup milk
Salt
1 cup coarse cornmeal
Black pepper
Good-quality olive oil for brushing
¾ cup freshly grated Parmesan cheese

1. Preparing the Ingredients
2. Generously grease an 8-inch square baking dish or standard loaf pan with butter. Combine the milk with 2 cups of water and a large pinch of salt in a medium saucepan over medium heat. Bring just about to a boil, then add the cornmeal in a steady stream, whisking constantly to prevent lumps from forming. Turn the heat down to low and simmer, whisking frequently, until it has the consistency of thick oatmeal, 10 to 15 minutes. Stir in the butter, taste, and adjust the seasoning with salt and pepper. Pour the polenta into the prepared pan and spread into an even layer. Let stand at room temperature until fully cooled, about 1 hour, or cover and refrigerate overnight.
3. Turn the polenta out onto a cutting board. With a serrated knife, cut it into 11/2- to 2-inch squares. Brush the squares with oil on both sides.
4. Bring the griddle to medium-high heat. Oil the griddle and allow it to heat until the oil is shimmering but not smoking. Put the polenta squares on the griddle and cook until they brown and are heated for 10 minutes. Transfer to a platter, immediately sprinkle with the Parmesan, and serve.

Nutrition: Calories: 74, Fat: 5.4 g, Protein: 10 g, Carbs: 6.1 g

Poultry Recipes

4 pounds of your favorite chicken, including legs, thighs, wings, and breasts, skin-on
Salt
Olive oil
1 cup barbecue sauce, like Hickory Mesquite or homemade

Classic BBQ Chicken

 Prep Time 5 min **Cook Time** 80 min **Servings** 1

1. Rub the chicken with olive oil and salt.
2. Preheat the griddle to high heat.
3. Sear chicken skin side down on the griddle for 5-10 minutes.
4. Turn the griddle down to medium-low heat, tent with foil, and cook for 30 minutes.
5. Turn chicken and baste with barbecue sauce.
6. Cover the chicken again and allow it to cook for another 20 minutes.
7. Baste, cover, and cook again for 30 minutes; repeat basting and turning during this time.
8. The chicken is done when the internal temperature of the chicken pieces is 165°F and the juices run clear.
9. Baste with more barbecue sauce to serving!

Nutrition: Calories: 539, Fat: 11 g, Carbs: 15 g, Protein: 87 g

Sweet Chili Lime Chicken

 Prep Time 10 min **Cook Time** 37 min **Servings** 2

1/2 cup sweet chili sauce
1/4 cup soy sauce
1 teaspoon mirin
1 teaspoon orange juice, fresh squeezed
1 teaspoon orange marmalade
2 tablespoons lime juice
1 tablespoon brown sugar
1 clove of garlic, minced
4 boneless, skinless chicken breasts
Sesame seeds, for garnish

1. Whisk sweet chili sauce, soy sauce, mirin, orange marmalade, lime and orange juice, brown sugar, and minced garlic together in a small mixing bowl.
2. Set aside 1/4 cup of the sauce.
3. Toss chicken in sauce to coat and marinate for 30 minutes.
4. Preheat your griddle to medium heat.
5. Put the chicken on the griddle and cook each side for 7 minutes.
6. Baste the cooked chicken with the remaining marinade and garnish with sesame seeds to serve with your favorite sides.

Nutrition: Calories: 380, Fat: 12 g, Carbs: 19 g, Protein: 43 g

Hasselback Stuffed Chicken

 Prep Time 15 min **Cook Time** 20 min **Servings** 4

4 boneless, skinless chicken breasts
2 tablespoons olive oil
2 tablespoons taco seasoning
1/2 red, yellow, and green pepper, very thinly sliced
1 small red onion, very thinly sliced
1/2 cup Mexican shredded cheese
Guacamole, for serving
Sour cream, for serving
Salsa, for serving

1. Preheat the griddle to med-high.
2. Cut thin horizontal cuts across each chicken breast, like you would Hasselback potatoes.
3. Rub chicken evenly with olive oil and taco seasoning.
4. Add a mixture of bell peppers and red onions to each cut, and place the breasts on the griddle.
5. Cook chicken for 15 minutes.
6. Remove and top with cheese.
7. Tent loosely with foil and cook another 5 minutes until cheese is melted.
8. Remove from the griddle and top with guacamole, sour cream, and salsa. Serving alongside your favorite side dishes!

Nutrition: Calories: 643, Fat: 18 g, Carbs: 26 g, Protein: 93 g

Salsa Verde Marinated Chicken

 Prep Time 26 min **Cook Time** 14 min **Servings** 6

6 boneless, skinless chicken breasts
1 tablespoon olive oil
1 teaspoon sea salt
1 teaspoon chili powder
1 teaspoon ground cumin
1 teaspoon garlic powder

For the salsa verde marinade:
3 teaspoons garlic, minced
1 small onion, chopped
6 tomatillos, husked, rinsed, and chopped
1 medium jalapeño pepper, cut in half, seeded
1/4 cup fresh cilantro, chopped
1/2 teaspoon sugar or sugar substitute

1. Add salsa verde marinade ingredients to a food processor and pulse until smooth.
2. Mix sea salt, chili powder, cumin, and garlic powder in a small mixing bowl. Season chicken breasts with olive oil and seasoning mix and lay in a glass baking dish.
3. Spread a tablespoon of salsa verde marinade over each chicken breast to cover, reserving the remaining salsa for serving.
4. Cover the dish with plastic wrap and refrigerate for 4 hours.
5. Preheat the griddle to medium-high and brush with olive oil.
6. Add chicken to the griddle and cook 7 minutes per side or until juices run clear and a meat thermometer reads 165°F.
7. Serving each with additional salsa verde and enjoy!

Nutrition: Calories: 125, Fat: 12 g, Carbs: 4 g, Protein: 2 g

Chicken Thighs with Ginger-Sesame Glaze

 Prep Time 25 min **Cook Time** 6 min **Servings** 8

8 boneless, skinless chicken thighs

For the glaze:
3 tablespoons dark brown sugar
2 1/2 tablespoons soy sauce
1 tablespoon fresh garlic, minced
2 teaspoons sesame seeds
1 teaspoon fresh ginger, minced
1 teaspoon sambal Oelek
1/3 cup scallions, thinly sliced
Non-stick cooking spray

1. Combine glaze ingredients in a large mixing bowl; separate and reserving half for serving.
2. Add chicken to bowl and toss to coat well.
3. Preheat the griddle to medium-high heat.
4. Coat with cooking spray.
5. Cook chicken for 6 minutes on each side or until done.
6. Transfer chicken to plates and drizzle with remaining glaze to serving.

Nutrition: Calories: 301, Fat: 11 g, Carbs: 4 g, Protein: 42 g

Seared Spicy Citrus Chicken

 Prep Time 10 min   **Cook Time** 14 min   **Servings** 2

1. Whisk together marinade ingredients in a large mixing bowl, reserving 2 tablespoons of the marinade for basting.
2. Add chicken and marinade to a sealable plastic bag and marinate for 8 hours or overnight in the refrigerator.
3. Preheat the griddle to medium-high heat and brush lightly with olive oil.
4. Place chicken on the griddle and cook 8 minutes per side.
5. Drizzle each side of chicken with reserved marinade for the last few minutes of cooking; chicken is done when the internal temperature reaches 165 ° F.
6. Place the chicken on a plate, cover it with aluminum foil and let it rest for 5 minutes.
7. Serve and enjoy!

2 lbs. boneless, skinless chicken thighs

For the marinade:
1/4 cup fresh lime juice
2 teaspoon lime zest
1/4 cup honey
2 tablespoons olive oil
1 tablespoon balsamic vinegar
1/2 teaspoon sea salt
1/2 teaspoon black pepper
2 garlic cloves, minced
1/4 teaspoon onion powder

Nutrition: Calories: 381, Fat: 20 g, Carbs: 4 g, Protein: 44 g

Creole Chicken Stuffed with Cheese and Peppers

 Prep Time 10 min   **Cook Time** 14 min   **Servings** 4

4 boneless, skinless chicken breasts
8 mini sweet peppers, sliced thin and seeded
2 slices pepper jack cheese, cut in half
2 slices Colby Jack cheese, cut in half
1 tablespoon creole seasoning, like Emeril's
1 teaspoon black pepper
1 teaspoon garlic powder
1 teaspoon onion powder
4 teaspoons olive oil, separated
Toothpicks

1. Rinse chicken and pat dry.
2. Mix creole seasoning, pepper, garlic powder, and onion powder in a small mixing bowl and set aside.
3. Cut a slit on the side of each chicken breast; be careful not to cut through the chicken.
4. Rub each breast with 1 teaspoon of olive oil.
5. Rub each chicken breast with seasoning mix and coat evenly.
6. Stuff each breast of chicken with 1 half pepper jack cheese slice, 1 half Colby cheese slice, and a handful of pepper slices.
7. Secure chicken shut with 4 or 5 toothpicks.
8. Preheat the griddle to medium-high and cook chicken for 8 minutes per side; or until chicken reaches an internal temperature of 165°F.
9. Allow chicken to rest for 5 minutes, remove toothpicks, and serve.

Nutrition: Calories: 509, Fat: 25 g, Carbs: 19 g, Protein: 51 g

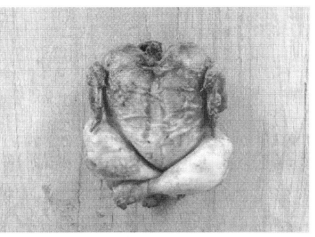

1 lb. boneless chicken thighs
3 can (12 ounces) root beer, like A&W
Olive oil

For the rub:
1 tablespoon garlic powder
3/4 tablespoon sea salt
1/2 tablespoon white pepper
2 teaspoons smoked paprika
2 teaspoons garlic powder
1 teaspoon dried thyme
1/8 teaspoon cayenne pepper

Root Beer Can Chicken

 Prep Time 10 min **Cook Time** 14 min **Servings** 2

1. Combine rub ingredients in a bowl; reserving half in a separate air-tight container until ready to cook.
2. Rub chicken thighs evenly with olive oil and coat each with some rub.
3. Lay chicken in a 13 by 9-inch baking dish. Cover with 2 cans of root beer.
4. Preheat the griddle to medium-high heat.
5. Discard marinade and brush the griddle with olive oil.
6. Gently fold the remaining rub and a half of the third can of root beer into a small bowl.
7. Sear chicken for 7 minutes on each side, basting often with root beer rub mix.
8. Serving when cooked through or the chicken reaches 165°F and juices run clear.

Nutrition: Calories: 363, Fat: 12 g, Carbs: 29 g, Protein: 33 g

Chicken Tacos with Avocado Crema

 Prep Time 25 min **Cook Time** 10 min **Servings** 3

1 1/2 lbs. Boneless, skinless chicken breasts, sliced thin

For the chicken marinade:
1 serrano pepper, minced
2 teaspoons garlic, minced
1 lime, juiced
1 teaspoon ground cumin
1/3 cup olive oil
Sea salt, to taste
Black pepper, to taste

For the avocado crema:
1 cup sour cream
2 teaspoons lime juice
1 teaspoon lime zest
1 serrano pepper, diced and seeded
1 clove of garlic, minced
1 large Hass avocado

For the garnish:
1/2 cup queso fresco, crumbled
2 teaspoons cilantro, chopped
1 lime sliced into wedges
10 corn tortillas

1. Mix chicken marinade in a sealable plastic bag. Add chicken and toss to coat well.
2. Marinate for 1 hour in the refrigerator.
3. Combine avocado crema ingredients in a food processor or blender and pulse until smooth.
4. Cover and refrigerate until you are ready to assemble tacos.
5. Preheat the griddle to medium heat and cook the chicken for 5 minutes per side, rotating and turning as needed.
6. Remove from the griddle and tent loosely with aluminum foil. Allow chicken to rest for 5 minutes.
7. Servings with warm tortillas, a dollop of avocado crema, queso fresco, cilantro, and lime wedges.
8. To meal prep: simply divide the chicken into individual portion containers with a serving of the garnish, and take with tortillas wrapped in parchment paper to warm in a microwave to serving.

Nutrition: Calories: 703, Fat: 44 g, Carbs: 30 g, Protein: 47 g

Fiery Italian Chicken Skewers

 Prep Time 5 min   **Cook Time** 10 min   **Servings** 10

10 boneless, skinless chicken thighs, cut into chunks
1 large red onion, cut into wedges
1 large red pepper, stemmed, seeded, and cut into chunks

For the marinade:
1/3 cup toasted pine nuts
1 1/2 cups sliced roasted red peppers
5 hot cherry peppers, stemmed and seeded, or to taste
1 cup packed fresh basil leaves, plus more for servings
4 cloves garlic, peeled
1/4 cup grated Parmesan cheese
1 tablespoon paprika
Extra virgin olive oil, as needed

1. Combine the toasted pine nuts, roasted red peppers, hot cherry peppers, basil, garlic, Parmesan, and paprika in a food processor or blender and process until well-combined.
2. Add in olive oil until the pesto reaches a thin consistency to coat the chicken as a marinade.
3. Transfer half of the pesto to a large sealable plastic bag and reserve the other half for serving.
4. Add the chicken thigh chunks to the bag of pesto, seal, and massage the bag to coat the chicken.
5. Refrigerate for 1 hour.
6. Preheat the griddle to medium-high heat and brush with olive oil.
7. Thread the chicken cubes, red onion, and red pepper onto metal skewers.
8. Brush the chicken with the reserved pesto.
9. Cook until the chicken reaches an internal temperature of 165°F; about 5 minutes per side. Serving warm with your favorite salad or vegetables!

Nutrition: Calories: 363, Fat: 12 g, Carbs: 29 g, Protein: 33 g

Classic BBQ Chicken Legs

 Prep Time 15 min   **Cook Time** 50 min   **Servings** 2

4 pounds legs, thighs
Salt, to taste
Olive oil
1 cup barbecue sauce

1. Rub the chicken with olive oil and salt.
2. Preheat the griddle to high heat.
3. Sear chicken skin side down on the griddle for 5 to 10 minutes.
4. Turn the griddle down to medium-low heat, tent with foil, and cook for 30 minutes.
5. Turn chicken and baste with barbecue sauce.
6. Cover the chicken again and allow it to cook for another 20 minutes.
7. Baste, cover, and cook again for 30 minutes; repeat basting and turning during this time.
8. The chicken is done when the internal temperature of the chicken pieces is 165°F (74°C), and the juices run clear.

Nutrition:Calories: 409, Fat: 28 g, Carbs: 26 g, Protein: 36 g

California Seared Chicken

 Prep Time 10 min   **Cook Time** 10 min   **Servings** 3

1. Whisk together balsamic vinegar, honey, olive oil, oregano, basil, and garlic powder in a large mixing bowl.

2. Add chicken to coat and marinate for 30 minutes in the refrigerator.

3. Preheat the griddle to medium-high. Sear chicken for 7 minutes per side, or until a meat thermometer reaches 165°F (74°C).

4. Top each chicken breast with mozzarella, avocado, tomato, and tent with foil on the griddle to melt for 2 minutes.

5. Garnish with a drizzle of balsamic glaze, and a pinch of sea salt and black pepper.

4 boneless, skinless chicken breasts
¾ cup balsamic vinegar
2 tablespoons extra virgin olive oil
1 tablespoon honey
1 teaspoon oregano
1 teaspoon basil
1 teaspoon garlic powder

For Garnish:
Sea salt
Black pepper, fresh ground
4 slices of fresh mozzarella cheese
4 slices avocado
4 slices beefsteak tomato
Balsamic glaze, for drizzling

Nutrition:Calories: 423, Fat: 18 g, Carbs: 9 g, Protein: 6 g

Honey Balsamic Marinated Chicken

 Prep Time 30 min   **Cook Time** 14 min   **Servings** 2

2 pounds (907 g) of boneless, skinless chicken thighs
1 teaspoon olive oil
1/2 teaspoon sea salt
1/4 teaspoon black pepper
1/2 teaspoon paprika
¾ teaspoon onion powder
For the Marinade:
2 tablespoons honey
2 tablespoons balsamic vinegar
2 tablespoons tomato paste
1 teaspoon garlic, minced

1. Add chicken, olive oil, salt, black pepper, paprika, and onion powder to a sealable plastic bag. Seal and toss to coat, covering the chicken with spices and oil; set aside.

2. Whisk together balsamic vinegar, tomato paste, garlic, and honey.

3. Divide the marinade in half. Add one half to the bag of chicken and store the other half in a sealed container in the refrigerator.

4. Seal the bag and toss chicken to coat. Refrigerate for 30 minutes to 4 hours.

5. Preheat a griddle to medium-high.

6. Discard bag and marinade. Add chicken to the griddle and cook 7 minutes per side or until juices run clear and a meat thermometer reads 165°F (74°C).

7. During the last minute of cooking, brush the remaining marinade on top of the chicken thighs and serve immediately.

Nutrition: Calories: 450, Fat: 18 g, Carbs: 6 g, Protein: 24 g

Hawaiian Chicken Skewers

 Prep Time 15 min **Cook Time** 30 min **Servings** 3

1 pound (454 g) boneless, skinless chicken breast, cut into 1 1/2 inch cubes
3 cups pineapple, cut into 1 1/2 inch cubes
2 large green peppers, cut into 1 1/2 inch pieces
1 large red onion, cut into 1 1/2 inch pieces
2 tablespoons olive oil to coat veggies

For Marinade:
1/3 cup tomato paste
1/3 cup brown sugar, packed
1/3 cup soy sauce
1/4 cup pineapple juice
2 tablespoons olive oil
1 1/2 tablespoon mirin or rice wine vinegar
4 teaspoons garlic cloves, minced
1 tablespoon ginger, minced
1/2 teaspoon sesame oil
Pinch of sea salt
Pinch of ground black pepper
10 wooden skewers for assembly

1. Combine marinade ingredients in a mixing bowl until smooth. Reserve a 1/2 cup of the marinade in the refrigerator.
2. Add chicken and remaining marinade to a sealable plastic bag and refrigerate for 1 hour.
3. Soak 10 wooden skewer sticks in water for 1 hour.
4. Preheat the griddle to medium heat.
5. Add red onion, bell pepper, and pineapple to a mixing bowl with 2 tablespoons olive oil and toss to coat.
6. Thread red onion, bell pepper, pineapple, and chicken onto the skewers until all of the chicken has been used.
7. Place skewers on the griddle and grab your reserved marinade from the refrigerator; cook for 5 minutes, brush with the remaining marinade, and rotate.
8. Brush again with marinade and sear for about 5 additional minutes or until the chicken reads 165°F (74°C) on a meat thermometer.
9. Serve warm.

Nutrition Calories: 290, Fat: 9 g, Carbs: 2 g, Protein: 13g

Sizzling Chicken Fajitas

 Prep Time 5 min **Cook Time** 14 min **Servings** 4

1. In a zipper-lock bag, combine the chicken, cumin, garlic, onion, lime juice, salt, pepper, and olive oil. Allow marinating for 30 minutes.
2. Preheat the griddle to medium heat.
3. On one side of the griddle, add the olive oil and heat until shimmering. Add the onion and pepper and cook until slightly softened.
4. On the other side of the griddle, add the marinated chicken and cook until lightly browned.
5. Once the chicken is lightly browned, toss together with the onion and pepper and cook until the chicken registers 165°F (74°C).
6. Remove chicken and vegetables from the griddle and serve with warm tortillas.

4 boneless chicken breast halves, thinly sliced
1 yellow onion, sliced
1 large green bell pepper, sliced
1 large red bell pepper, sliced
1 teaspoon ground cumin
1 teaspoon garlic powder
1 teaspoon onion powder
2 tablespoons lime juice
1 tablespoon olive oil
1/2 teaspoon black pepper
1 teaspoon salt
3 tablespoons vegetable oil
10 flour tortillas

Nutrition:Calories: 602, Fat: 12 g, Carbs: 8 g, Protein: 21 g

Chipotle Adobe Chicken

 Prep Time 10 min **Cook Time** 24 min **Servings** 2

2 pounds (907 g) of chicken thighs or breasts (boneless, skinless)

For the Marinade:
1/4 cup olive oil
2 chipotle peppers, in adobo sauce, plus 1 teaspoon of adobo sauce from the can
1 tablespoon garlic, minced
1 shallot, finely chopped
11/2 tablespoons cumin
1 tablespoon cilantro, super-finely chopped or dried
2 teaspoons chili powder
1 teaspoon dried oregano
1/2 teaspoon salt
Fresh limes, garnish
Cilantro, garnish

1. Preheat the griddle to medium-high.
2. Add marinade ingredients to a food processor or blender and pulse into a paste.
3. Add the chicken and marinade to a sealable plastic bag and massage to coat well.
4. Place in the refrigerator for 1 hour to 24 hours before cooking.
5. Sear chicken for 7 minutes, turn and cook for additional 7 minutes.
6. Turn heat to low and cook until the chicken has reached an internal temperature of 165°F (74°C).
7. Remove chicken from griddle and allow to rest 5 to 10 minutes before serving.
8. Garnish with a squeeze of fresh lime and a sprinkle of cilantro to serve

Nutrition: Calories: 331, Fats: 23 g, Carbs: 4 g, Protein: 24 g

Chicken with Mustard

 Prep Time 15 min   **Cook Time** 50 min **Servings** 8

2 (3- to 4-pound / 1.4- to 1.8-kg) whole chickens

For the Brine:
1/2 cup salt
1/2 cup sugar
8 cups water
Toasted Mustard Seed Oil, for coating
Salt and pepper, for coating

1. Preheat the griddle to medium-high heat.
2. To prepare each chicken, using kitchen shears, cut along both sides of the backbone and remove (your butcher can also do this for you). Place the chicken skin side up on the cutting board and apply firm pressure to the breastbone to flatten.
3. To make the brine: Combine the salt, sugar, and water and stir until dissolved. In a large bowl or stockpot, submerge the chickens in the liquid and refrigerate, covered, for at least 4 hours or up to overnight. Remove and pat dry.
4. Coat the chickens with the mustard seed oil, salt, and pepper and cook, bone side down, over high heat for about 10 minutes. Flip the chickens, move to medium heat, and cook for another 30 minutes, or until an instant-read meat thermometer placed in the thickest part of the thigh reads 165°F (74°C). Flip the chickens occasionally and baste with more mustard seed oil, if needed. Transfer to a cutting board and let the chickens rest for 10 minutes before carving into serving pieces.

Nutrition: Calories: 637, Fat: 29 g, Carbs: 25 g, Protein: 64 g

Buffalo Chicken Wings

Prep Time 15 min **Cook Time** 22 min **Servings** 4

1 tablespoon sea salt
1 teaspoon ground black pepper
1 teaspoon garlic powder
3 pounds (1.4 kg) of chicken wings
6 tablespoons unsalted butter
1/3 cup buffalo sauce, like Moore's
1 tablespoon apple cider vinegar
1 tablespoon honey

1. Combine salt, pepper, and garlic powder in a large mixing bowl.
2. Toss the wings with the seasoning mixture to coat.
3. Preheat the griddle to medium heat.
4. Place the wings on the griddle; make sure they touch and the meat stays moist on the bone while cooking.
5. Flip wings every 5 minutes, for a total of 20 minutes of cooking.
6. Heat the butter, buffalo sauce, vinegar, and honey in a saucepan over low heat; whisk to combine well.
7. Add wings to a large mixing bowl, and toss them with the sauce to coat.
8. Turn the griddle up to medium-high and place wings back on the griddle until the skins crisp; about 1 to 2 minutes per side.
9. Add wings back into the bowl with the sauce and toss to serve.

Nutrition: Calories: 410, Fat: 21 g, Carbs: 2 g, Protein: 49 g

Korean Griddled Chicken Wings with Scallion

Prep Time 10 min **Cook Time** 17 min **Servings** 4

2 pounds (907 g) of chicken wings (flats and drumettes attached or separated)
For the Marinade:
1 tablespoon olive oil
1 teaspoon sea salt, plus more
1/2 teaspoon black pepper
1/2 cup Gochujang, Korean hot pepper paste
1 scallion, thinly sliced, for garnish

1. Rinse and pat the wings dry with paper towels.
2. Whisk marinade ingredients together in a large mixing bowl until well-combined.
3. Add wings to bowl and toss to coat.
4. Cover bowl with plastic wrap and chill in the refrigerator for 30 minutes.
5. Prepare one side of the griddle for medium heat and the other side for medium-high.
6. Working in batches, cook wings over medium heat, turning occasionally, until the skin starts to brown; about 12 minutes.
7. Move wings to the medium-high area of the griddle for 5 minutes on each side to sear until cooked through; the meat thermometer should register 165°F (74°C) when touching the bone.
8. Transfer wings to a platter, garnish with scallions and serve warm with your favorite dipping sauces.

Nutrition: Calories: 121, Protein: 12 g, Carbs: 1 g, Fat: 8 g

Griddled BBQ Chicken Wings

Prep Time 5 min **Cook Time** 18 min **Servings** 7

4 lbs. chicken wings or drumettes
1/2 cup baking powder
2 minced garlic cloves
1 teaspoon salt to taste
1 teaspoon black pepper to taste
1 cup barbecue sauce
Lime wedges for serving

1. Place the chicken wings in a plastic or Ziploc bag, add the baking powder, garlic, pepper, and salt to taste, then shake to coat. This will help you get crispy chicken wings when griddled. Let the chicken rest for about 15 minutes, then set aside.
2. Preheat the griddle to 275 to 300°F, place chicken wings on it, and cook for about six to ten minutes. Flip the chicken side to side, over, and cook for another five to six minutes until it is cooked through and attains an internal temperature of 185°F.
3. Glaze the wings with the barbeque sauce, cook for another two minutes, then serve with lime wedges.

Nutrition: Calories: 429, Carbs: 35 g, Fat: 30 g, Protein: 31 g

Asian Honey Chicken

 Prep Time 5 min **Cook Time** 9 min **Servings** 4

1. Heat the griddle pan to medium and brush with oil.
2. Place all ingredients in a bowl and mix until the chicken breasts are well-seasoned.
3. Place the seasoned chicken breasts on the hot griddle pan and cook for 6 to 9 minutes on each side.

1 tbs Olive oil
4 boneless chicken breasts
2 tablespoons soy sauce
2 tablespoons honey
1 tablespoon lemon juice
1/4tsp ground black pepper
Salt to taste

Nutrition: Calories: 558, Protein: 61 g, Carbs: 11 g, Fat: 29 g

Sweet Red Chili and Peach Glaze Wings

 Prep Time 10 min **Cook Time** 30 min **Servings** 2

1. Mix peach preserves, red chili sauce, lime juice, and cilantro in a mixing bowl. Divide in half, and place one half aside for serving.
2. Preheat the griddle to medium heat and spray with non-stick cooking spray.
3. Cook wings for 25 minutes, turning several times until juices run clear.
4. Remove wings from the griddle, and toss in a bowl to coat wings with the remaining glaze.
5. Return wings to griddle and cook for an additional 3 to 5 minutes, turning once.
6. Serve warm with your favorite dips and side dishes!

1 (12-ounce / 340-g) jar peach preserves
1 cup sweet red chili sauce
1 teaspoon lime juice
1 tablespoon fresh cilantro, minced
1 (21/2-pound / 1.1-kg) bag chicken wing sections
Non-stick cooking spray

Nutrition: Calories: 390, Fat: 73 g, Carbs: 42 g, Protein: 65 g

Yellow Curry Chicken Wings

Prep Time 5 min

Cook Time 13 min

Servings 4

2 pounds (907 g) of chicken wings

For the marinade:
1/2 cup Greek yogurt, plain
1 tablespoon mild yellow curry powder
1 tablespoon olive oil
1/2 teaspoon sea salt
1/2 teaspoon black pepper
1 teaspoon red chili flakes

1. Rinse and pat the wings dry with paper towels.
2. Whisk marinade ingredients together in a large mixing bowl until well-combined.
3. Add wings to bowl and toss to coat.
4. Cover bowl with plastic wrap and chill in the refrigerator for 30 minutes. Prepare one side of the griddle for medium heat and the other side for medium-high.
5. Working in batches, cook the wings over medium heat, turning occasionally, until the skin starts to brown; about 12 minutes.
6. Move wings to the medium-high area of the griddle for 5 minutes on each side to char until cooked through; the meat thermometer should register 165°F (74°C) when touching the bone.
7. Transfer wings to a platter and serve warm.

Nutrition: Calories: 213, Fat: 6 g, Carbs: 5 g, Protein: 20 g

Roasted Tuscan Thighs

Prep Time 10 min

Cook Time 75 min

Servings 8

8 chicken thighs, with bone, with skin
3 extra virgin olive oils with roasted garlic flavor
3 cups of Tuscan or Tuscan seasoning per thigh

1. Cut off excess skin-on chicken thighs and leave at 1/4 inch to shrink.
2. Carefully peel off the skin and remove large deposits of Fat: under the skin and behind the thighs.
3. Lightly rub olive oil behind and below the skin and thighs. A seasoning from Tuscan, seasoned on the skin of the thigh and the top and bottom of the back.
4. Wrap chicken thighs in plastic wrap, refrigerate for 1-2 hours and allow time for flavor to be absorbed before roasting.
5. Preheat the griddle to 375°F.
6. Roast for 40-60 minutes until the internal temperature of the thick part of the chicken thigh reaches 180°F. Place the roasted Tuscan thighs under a loose foil tent for 15 minutes before serving.

Nutrition: Calories: 260, Carbs: 1 g, Fat: 20 g, Protein: 19 g

Lemon Cornish Chicken Stuffed with Crab

 Prep Time 10 min   **Cook Time** 20 min   **Servings** 2

2 Cornish chickens (about 1¾ pound each)
Half lemon
4 tablespoons western rub or poultry rub
2 cups stuffed with crab meat

1. Rinse chicken thoroughly inside and outside, tap lightly and let it dry.
2. Carefully loosen the skin on the chest and legs. Rub the lemon under and over the skin and into the cavity. Rub the western lab under and over the skin on the chest and legs. Carefully return the skin to its original position.
3. Wrap the Cornish hen in plastic wrap and refrigerate for 2-3 hours until the flavor is absorbed.
4. Prepare crab meat stuffing according to the instructions. Make sure it is completely cooled before packing the chicken. Loosely fill the cavities of each hen with crab filling.
5. Tie the Cornish chicken legs with a butcher's leash to put the filling.
6. Preheat the griddle to 375°F.
7. Place the stuffed animal on the rack in the baking dish. If you do not have a rack that is small enough to fit, you can also place the chicken directly on the baking dish.
8. Roast the chicken at 375°F until the inside temperature of the thickest part of the chicken breast reaches 170°F, the thigh reaches 180°F, and the juice is clear.
9. Test the crab meat stuffing to see if the temperature has reached 165°F.
10. Place the roasted chicken under a loose foil tent for 15 minutes before serving.

Nutrition: Calories: 275, Carbs: 0 g, Fat: 3 g, Protein: 32 g

Cajun Patch Cock Chicken

 Prep Time 10 min   **Cook Time** 120 min   **Servings** 8

4-5 pounds of fresh or thawed frozen chicken
4-6 glasses of extra virgin olive oil
4 tablespoons Cajun spice lab or Lucile bloody Mary mix Cajun hot dry herb mix seasoning

1. Place the chicken breast on a cutting board with the chest down.
2. Using kitchen or poultry scissors, cut along the side of the spine and remove.
3. Turn your chicken side to side, over, and press down firmly on the chest to flatten it. Carefully loosen and remove the skin on the chest, thighs, and drumsticks.
4. Rub olive oil freely under and on the skin. Season chicken in all directions and apply directly to the meat under the skin.
5. Wrap the chicken in plastic wrap and place it in the refrigerator for 3 hours to absorb the flavor.
6. Preheat the griddle to 225°F.
7. Cook the chicken for 1.5 hours.
8. After one and a half hours at 225°F, raise the pit temperature to 375°F and roast until the inside temperature of the thickest part of the chest reaches 170°F, and the thighs are at least 180°F.
9. Place the chicken under a loose foil tent for 15 minutes before carving.

Nutrition: Calories: 390, Fat: 73 g, Carbs: 42 g, Protein: 65 g

Griddled Chicken Satay

 Prep Time 5 min   **Cook Time** 15 min   **Servings** 7

1. Properly slice the chicken as desired, preferably lengthwise, then add to a Ziploc bag, and set aside. Using a large mixing bowl, add the milk, fish sauce, soy sauce, lime juice, garlic powder, cayenne pepper, salt, and pepper to taste, then mix properly to combine. Pour the marinade into the resealable bag, then shake properly to coat, and refrigerate for about thirty minutes to three hours.

2. To make the dipping sauce, place all its ingredients in a mixing bowl, then mix properly to combine, and set aside. Preheat the griddle to 350°F, thread the chicken onto skewers, then place the skewers on the preheated griddle.

3. Cook the chicken satay for about ten to fifteen minutes until it reads 165°F. Make sure you flip the chicken occasionally as you cook. Serve with the prepared dipping sauce and enjoy.

Marinade:
1 1/2 pounds boneless and skinless chicken breasts or thighs
3/4 cup coconut milk
2 tablespoons fish sauce
2 tablespoons soy sauce
2 tablespoons lime juice
1/2 teaspoon kosher salt to taste
1/2 teaspoon black pepper to taste
1/2 teaspoon garlic powder
1/4 teaspoon cayenne pepper

Dipping sauce:
1/2 cup coconut milk
1/3 cup peanut butter
2 minced garlic cloves
1 tablespoon soy sauce
1 teaspoon fish sauce
1 tablespoon lime juice
1/2 tablespoon swerve sweetener
1 tablespoon sriracha hot sauce
1 cup chopped cilantro

Nutrition: Calories: 488, Fat: 32 g, Carbs: 10 g, Protein: 41 g

63

Vinegary Chicken with Mustard

 Prep Time 10 min   **Cook Time** 30 min   **Servings** 8

2 (3- to 4-pound / 1.4- to 1.8-kg) whole chickens
2 cups pickled mustard seeds
1/4 cup vinegar
3 tablespoons honey, plus more for basting and*to taste
2 teaspoons salt, plus more for seasoning

1. Preheat the griddle to medium-high heat.
2. To prepare each chicken, using kitchen shears, cut along both sides of the backbone and remove (your butcher can also do this for you). Place the chicken skin side up on the cutting board and apply firm pressure to the breastbone to flatten.
3. Add 1 cup of the mustard seeds to a blender together with the vinegar, 1 tablespoon of the honey, and the salt, and blend until smooth. Toss the chicken with the marinade and refrigerate, covered, for at least 2 hours or up to overnight. Remove the chicken from the marinade, wipe off any excess, and discard the marinade.
4. Cook the chickens, bone side down, over high heat for about 10 minutes. Flip the chickens, move to medium heat, and cook for another 30 minutes, or until an instant-read meat thermometer placed in the thickest part of the thigh reads 165°F (74°C). You can flip the chickens occasionally while cooking to give them even color. During the last 5 minutes of cooking, brush them with honey. Transfer to a cutting board and let the chickens rest for 10 minutes before carving into serving pieces.
5. While the chickens are cooking, add the remaining 1 cup mustard seeds and the remaining 2 tablespoons honey to the blender and blend until smooth. Add additional honey and/or salt, if needed. To serve, smear the mustard seed puree on a large platter (or on 4 individual plates) and top with the chicken.

Nutrition: Calories: 310, Protein: 11 g, Carbs: 67 g, Fat: 1 g

2 teaspoons baking powder
1 cup shredded Cheddar cheese
1 1/2 lbs. chicken breast
2 eggs
3/4 cup almond flour
1 1/2 teaspoon lemon juice
1 small and sliced
3 tablespoons mayonnaise
1 tbs Olive oil
2 tablespoons chopped parsley
2 teaspoons chicken seasoning
1 tablespoon chopped scallions
2 tablespoons sour cream
1 chopped yellow onion
1/3 cup almond milk

Nutrition: Calories: 190, Fat: 14 g, Carbs: 7 g, Protein: 9 g

Delicious Chicken Fritters

 Prep Time 10 min **Cook Time** 10 min **Servings** 2

1. Preheat the griddle to 425°F, rub the chicken with olive oil, then season with half of the chicken seasoning. Place the seasoned chicken on the preheated griddle and cook for about twenty-five minutes until it attains an internal temperature of 165°F.

2. Let the cooked chicken rest for a few minutes, pull into smaller pieces with a fork, and add it into a large mixing bowl. Add in other ingredients like the onion, tomato, eggs, parsley, milk, and cheese, then mix everything to combine, and set aside.

3. In another mixing bowl, add the rest of the chicken seasoning, flour, and baking powder, then mix properly to combine. Pour the mixture into the bowl containing the pulled chicken mixture, then mix everything properly to combine. Cover the mixing bowl with plastic wrap, then refrigerate for about two hours.

4. Using another mixing bowl, add the mayonnaise, sour cream, scallions, parsley, and lemon juice, then mix properly to combine. This makes the serving dip. Feel free to store the dip in the refrigerator until ready to be served.

5. Preheat the griddle to medium-low flame, then grease the griddle with oil. Make fitters shape out of the chicken mixture, place the fritters on the preheated griddle, and cook for about three to four minutes. Flip the fritters over and cook for another three to four minutes, then serve with the dip.

Yan's Griddled Quarters

 Prep Time 30 min **Cook Time** 75 min **Servings** 4

4 fresh or thawed frozen chicken quarters
4-6 glasses of extra virgin olive oil
4 tablespoons of Yang's original dry lab

1. Cut off excess skin and Fat: chicken. Carefully peel the chicken skin and rub olive oil above and below each chicken skin.

2. In Jean's original dry lab, apply seasonings to the top and bottom of the skin and the back of the chicken house.

3. Wrap the seasoned chicken in plastic wrap and store refrigerated for 2-4 hours to absorb flavor.

4. Preheat the griddle to 325°F.

5. Place chicken on the griddle and cook at 325°F for 1 hour.

6. After one hour, raise the pit temperature to 400°F to finish the chicken and crisp the skin.

7. When the inside temperature of the thickest part of the thighs and feet reaches 180°F, and the juice becomes clear, pull the crispy chicken out of the griddle.

8. Let the crispy griddled chicken rest under a loose foil tent for 15 minutes before eating.

Nutrition: Calories: 250, Carbs: 0 g, Fat: 12 g, Protein: 21 g

Turkey Recipes

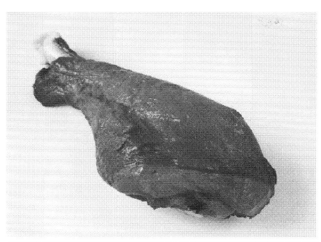

Turkey Legs

 Prep Time
20 min

 Cook Time
5 hours

 Servings
4

1. Prepare the brine and for this, take a large stockpot, place it over high heat, pour warm water in it, add peppercorn, bay leaves, and liquid smoke
2. Stir in salt, sugar, and BBQ rub and bring it to a boil.
3. Remove pot from heat, bring it to room temperature, then pour in cold water, add ice cubes and let the brine chill in the refrigerator. Then add turkey legs to it, submerge them completely, and let soak for 24 hours in the refrigerator.
4. After 24 hours, remove turkey legs from the brine, rinse well and pat dry with paper towels.
5. When ready to cook, switch on the griddle, set the temperature to 250°F, and let it preheat for a minimum of 15 minutes.
6. When the griddle has preheated, open the lid, place turkey legs on the griddle grate, shut the griddle, and cook for 5 hours until nicely browned and the internal temperature reaches 165°F. Serve immediately.

Nutrition: Calories: 416, Fat: 13 g, Carbs: 0 g, Protein: 69 g

For the Brine:
1/2 cup curing salt
1 tablespoon whole black peppercorns
1 cup BBQ rub
1/2 cup brown sugar
2 bay leaves
2 teaspoons liquid smoke
16 cups of warm water
4 cups ice
8 cups of cold water

Herb Roasted Turkey

 Prep Time
20 min

 Cook Time
4 hours

 Servings
8

14 pounds turkey, cleaned
2 tablespoons chopped mixed herbs
Pork and poultry rub as needed
1/4 teaspoon ground black pepper
3 tablespoons butter, unsalted, melted
8 tablespoons butter, unsalted, softened
2 cups chicken broth

1. Clean the turkey by removing the giblets, wash it inside out, pat dry with paper towels, then place it on a roasting pan and tuck the turkey wings by tiring with butcher's string.
2. Switch on the griddle, set the temperature to 325°F, and let it preheat for a minimum of 15 minutes.
3. Meanwhile, prepare herb butter and for this, take a small bowl, place the softened butter in it, add black pepper and mixed herbs and beat until fluffy.
4. Place some of the prepared herb butter underneath the skin of the turkey by using a handle of a wooden spoon, and massage the skin to distribute butter evenly.
5. Then rub the exterior of the turkey with melted butter, season with pork and poultry rub, and pour the broth into the roasting pan. When the griddle has preheated, open the lid, place the roasting pan containing turkey on the griddle grate, shut the griddle, and cook for 3 hours and 30 minutes until the internal temperature reaches 165°F and the top has turned golden brown.
6. When done, transfer the turkey to a cutting board, let it rest for 30 minutes, then carve it into slices and serve.

Nutrition: Calories: 154, Fat: 3 g, Carbs: 8 g, Protein: 29 g

Turkey Breast

Prep Time 20 min

Cook Time 8 h & 10 min

Servings 4

1. Prepare the brine and for this, take a large bowl, add salt, black pepper, and sugar in it, pour in water, and stir until sugar has dissolved. Place turkey breast in it, submerge it completely, and let it soak for a minimum of 12 hours in the refrigerator.

2. Meanwhile, Prepare the BBQ rub and for this, take a small bowl, place all of its ingredients in it and then stir until combined, set aside until required. Then remove turkey breast from the brine and season well with the Prepared BBQ rub. When ready to cook, switch on the griddle, set the temperature to 180°F, and let it preheat for a minimum of 15 minutes. When the griddle has been preheated, open the lid, place the turkey breast on it, change the temperature to 225°F, and cook for 8 hours.

3. When done, transfer the turkey to a cutting board, let it rest for 10 minutes, then cut it into slices and serve.

Nutrition: Calories: 250, Fat: 5 g, Carbs: 31 g, Protein: 18 g

For the Brine:
2 pounds turkey breast, deboned
2 tablespoons ground black pepper
1/4 cup salt
1 cup brown sugar
4 cups cold water

For the BBQ Rub:
2 tablespoons dried onions
2 tablespoons garlic powder
1/4 cup paprika
2 tablespoons ground black pepper
1 tablespoon salt
2 tablespoons brown sugar
2 tablespoons red chili powder
1 tablespoon cayenne pepper
2 tablespoons sugar
2 tablespoons ground cumin

Griddled Whole Turkey

Prep Time 20 min

Cook Time 7 hours

Servings 4

1. Supply your griddle following the manufacturer's specific start-up procedure. Preheat with the lid closed to 250°F.

2. Rub the turkey with oil and season with the poultry seasoning inside and out, getting under the skin.

3. In a bowl, combine the melted butter, apple juice, sage, and thyme to use for basting.

4. Put the turkey in a roasting pan, place it on the griddle, close the lid, and griddle for 5 to 6 hours, basting every hour until the skin is brown and crispy, or until a meat thermometer is inserted in the thickest part of the thigh reads 165°F.

5. Let the turkey meat rest for about 15 to 20 minutes before carving.

1 (10- to 12-pound) turkey, giblets removed
Extra-virgin olive oil, for rubbing
1/4 cup poultry seasoning
8 tablespoons (1 stick) unsalted butter, melted
1/2 cup apple juice
2 teaspoons dried sage
2 teaspoons dried thyme

Nutrition: Calories: 180, Carbs: 3 g, Fat: 2 g, Protein: 39 g

Zesty Basil Crusted Turkey

Salt and pepper for taste
1 pound boneless, skinless turkey meat, cut into bite-sized pieces
1 red bell pepper, washed and diced
8 ounces mushrooms, cleaned and sliced
2 cups zucchini or other summer squash (washed, stemmed, and sliced)
3 garlic cloves (minced or pressed)
8 ounces fresh basil (chopped)

 Prep Time 20 min Cook Time 20 min Servings 7

1. Preheat the griddle to high.
2. Season the turkey with salt and pepper for taste.
3. Add the turkey to the griddle, cooking on both sides until brown.
4. Pour in the rest of the ingredients and cook for 3 minutes.

Nutrition: Calories: 550, Fat: 33 g, Carbs: 9 g, Fat: 16 g

Turkey and Broccoli Stir Fry

 Prep Time 20 min Cook Time 20 min Servings 8

1 lb. turkey breast, skinless, boneless, and cut into chunks
1 tablespoon soy sauce
1 tablespoon ginger, minced
1/2 teaspoons garlic powder
1 tablespoon olive oil
1/2 onion, sliced
2 cups broccoli florets
2 teaspoons hot sauce
2 teaspoons vinegar
1 teaspoon sesame oil
Pepper
Salt

1. Add all ingredients into the large mixing bowl and toss well.
2. Preheat the griddle to medium heat.
3. Spray griddle top with cooking spray.
4. Transfer turkey and broccoli mixture onto the hot griddle top and cook until broccoli is tender and turkey is cooked.
5. Serve and enjoy.

Nutrition: Calories: 200, Fat: 7 g, Carbs: 6 g, Protein: 26 g

Lemony Turkey Paillards with Asparagus and Feta

 Prep Time 25 min Cook Time 10 min Servings 8

1 pound thin asparagus
1 tablespoon good-quality olive oil, plus more for brushing
Salt and pepper
1 1/2 pounds boneless, skinless turkey breasts, cut and pounded into paillards
1/2 cup crumbled feta cheese
Lemon wedges for serving

1. Preparing the Ingredients.
2. Cut off the bottoms of the asparagus, then toss the spears with 1 tablespoon oil and sprinkle with salt. Put them on the griddle and cook, turning once, until browned and crisp-tender, 3 to 5 Minutes. Transfer to a plate.
3. Brush the paillards with oil and sprinkle with salt and pepper on both sides. Put them on the griddle and cook, turning once, until the chicken is no longer pink in the center, 2 to 3 minutes per side. (Nick with a small knife and peek inside.) Transfer to individual plates, top with the asparagus, sprinkle with feta and serve with the lemon wedges.

Nutrition: Calories: 289, Fat: 12 g, Carbs: 18 g, Protein: 6 g

Turkey Jerky

Prep Time 25 min **Cook Time** 5 hours **Servings** 9

Marinade:
1 cup pineapple juice
1/2 cup brown sugar
2 tablespoons sriracha
2 teaspoons onion powder
2 tablespoons minced garlic
2 tablespoons rice wine vinegar
2 tablespoons hoisin
1 tablespoon red pepper flakes
1 tablespoon coarsely ground black pepper flakes
2 cups coconut amino
2 jalapenos (thinly sliced)

Meat:
3 pounds turkey boneless skinless breasts (sliced to 1/4 inch thick)

1. Pour the marinade mixture ingredients into a container and mix until the ingredients are well combined. Put the turkey slices in a gallon-sized zip-lock bag and pour the marinade into the bag. Massage the marinade into the turkey. Seal the bag and refrigerate for 8 hours.
2. Remove the turkey slices from the marinade.
3. Activate the griddle for smoking for 5 minutes until the fire starts.
4. Close the lid and preheat your griddle to 180°F.
5. Remove the turkey slices from the marinade and pat them dry with a paper towel.
6. Arrange the turkey slices on the griddle in a single layer. Cook the turkey for about 3 to 4 hours, turning often after the first 2 hours of smoking. The jerky should be dark and dry when it is done.
7. Remove the jerky from the griddle and let it sit for about 1 hour to cool. Serve immediately or store in the refrigerator.

Nutrition: Calories: 109, Carbs: 12 g, Fat: 1 g, Protein: 14 g

---

Jalapeno Injection Turkey

Prep Time 5 min **Cook Time** 15 min **Servings** 2

15 pounds whole turkey, giblet removed
1/2 of medium red onion, peeled and minced
8 jalapeño peppers
2 tablespoons minced garlic
4 tablespoons garlic powder
6 tablespoons Italian seasoning
1 cup butter, softened, unsalted
1/4 cup olive oil
1 cup chicken broth

1. Open the hopper of the griddle, add dry pallets, make sure the ash-can is in place, then open the ash damper, power on the griddle, and close the ash damper.
2. Make the temperature of the griddle up to 200°F. Let preheat for 30 minutes or until the green light on the dial blinks that indicate the griddle has reached to set temperature.
3. Meanwhile, place a large saucepan over medium-high heat, add oil and butter and when the butter melts, add onion, garlic, and peppers and cook for 3 to 5 minutes or until nicely golden brown.
4. Pour in broth, stir well, let the mixture boil for 5 minutes, then remove the pan from the heat and strain the mixture to get just liquid.
5. Inject turkey generously with prepared liquid, then spray the outside of turkey with butter spray and season well with garlic and Italian seasoning.
6. Place turkey on the griddle, shut with a lid, and cook for 30 minutes, then increase the temperature to 325°F and continue smoking the turkey for 3 hours or until the internal temperature of the turkey reaches 165°F.
7. When done, transfer turkey to a cutting board, let rest for 5 minutes, then carve into slices and serve.

Nutrition: Calories: 131, Fat: 7 g, Protein: 13 g, Carbs: 3 g

Whole Turkey

 Prep Time 10 min   **Cook Time** 4 hours   **Servings** 8

1 frozen whole turkey, giblets removed, thawed
2 tablespoons orange zest
2 tablespoons chopped fresh parsley
1 teaspoon salt
2 tablespoons chopped fresh rosemary
1 teaspoon ground black pepper
2 tablespoons chopped fresh sage
1 cup butter, unsalted, softened, divided
2 tablespoons chopped fresh thyme
1/2 cup water
14.5-ounce chicken broth

Nutrition: Calories: 146, Fat: 8 g, Protein: 18 g, Carbs: 1 g

1. Open the hopper of the griddle, add dry pallets, make sure the ash-can is in place, then open the ash damper, power on the griddle, and close the ash damper.
2. Set the temperature of the griddle to 180°F, and let preheat for 30 minutes or until the green light on the dial blinks – that indicates the griddle has reached to set temperature.
3. Meanwhile, prepare the turkey and for this, tuck its wings under it by using kitchen twine.
4. Place 1/2 cup butter in a bowl, add thyme, parsley, sage, orange zest, and rosemary, stir well until combined, then brush this mixture generously on the inside and outside of the turkey, and season the external of turkey with salt and black pepper.
5. Place turkey on a roasting pan, breast side up, pour in broth and water, add the remaining butter in the pan, then place the pan on the griddle and shut with a lid.
6. Cook the turkey for 3 hours, then increase the temperature to 350°F and continue smoking the turkey for 4 hours or until thoroughly cooked and the internal temperature of the turkey reaches 165°F, basting the turkey with the dripping every 30 minutes, but not in the last hour.
7. When you are done, take off the roasting pan from the griddle and let the turkey rest for 20 minutes.
8. Carve turkey into pieces and serve.

Marinated Griddled Turkey Breast

 Prep Time 25 min   **Cook Time** 4 h 15 min   **Servings** 4

1 (5 pounds) boneless chicken breast
4 cups water
2 tablespoons kosher salt
1 teaspoon Italian seasoning
2 tablespoons honey
1 tablespoon cider vinegar

Rub:
1/2 teaspoon onion powder
1 teaspoon paprika
1 teaspoon salt
1 teaspoon ground black pepper
1 tablespoon brown sugar
1/2 teaspoon garlic powder
1 teaspoon oregano

1. In a huge container, combine the water, honey, cider vinegar, Italian seasoning, and salt.
2. Add the chicken breast and toss to combine. Cover the bowl and place it in the refrigerator, and chill for 4 hours.
3. Rinse the chicken breast with water and pat dry with paper towels.
4. In another mixing bowl, combine the brown sugar, salt, paprika, onion powder, pepper, oregano, and garlic.
5. Generously season the chicken breasts with the rub mix.
6. Preheat the griddle to 225°F with the lid closed for 15 minutes.
7. Arrange the turkey breast into a griddle rack. Place the griddle rack on the griddle.
8. Cook for about 3 to 4 hours or until the internal temperature of the turkey breast reaches 165°F.
9. Remove the chicken breast from heat and let them rest for a few minutes. Serve.

Nutrition: Calories: 903, Fat: 34 g, Carbs: 9 g, Protein: 131 g

7 pounds turkey breast, bone-in, skin-on, Fat: trimmed
3/4 cup salt
1/3 cup brown sugar
4 quarts of water, cold

For Herbed Butter:
1 tablespoon chopped parsley
1/2 teaspoon ground black pepper
8 tablespoons butter, unsalted, softened
1 tablespoon chopped sage
1/2 tablespoon minced garlic
1 tablespoon chopped rosemary
1 teaspoon lemon zest
1 tablespoon chopped oregano
1 tablespoon lemon juice

Nutrition: Calories: 146, Fat: 8 g, Protein: 18 g, Carbs: 1 g

Herbed Turkey Breast

 Prep Time 25 min   **Cook Time** 2 hours   **Servings** 10

1. Prepare the brine and for this, pour water into a large container, add salt and sugar and stir well until salt and sugar have completely dissolved.
2. Add turkey breast to the brine, cover with the lid and let soak in the refrigerator for a minimum of 8 hours.
3. Then remove turkey breast from the brine, rinse well and pat dry with paper towels.
4. Open the hopper of the griddle, add dry pallets, make sure the ash-can is in place, then open the ash damper, power on the griddle, and close the ash damper.
5. Set the temperature of the griddle to 350°F, and let preheat for 30 minutes or until the green light on the dial blinks.
6. Meanwhile, take a roasting pan, pour in 1 cup of water, then place a wire rack in it and place turkey breast on it. Prepare the herb butter and for this, place butter in a heatproof bowl, add the remaining ingredients for the butter, and stir until just mixed.
7. Loosen the skin of the turkey from its breast by using your fingers, then insert 2 tablespoons of Prepared herb butter on each side of the skin of the breastbone and spread it evenly, pushing out all the air pockets.
8. Place the remaining herb butter in the bowl into the microwave wave and heat for 1 minute or more at a high heat setting or until melted. Then brush melted herb butter on the outside of the turkey breast and place a roasting pan containing turkey on the griddle.
9. Shut the griddle with a lid and cook for 2 hours and 30 minutes or until the turkey breast is nicely golden brown and the internal temperature of the turkey reaches 165°F, flipping the turkey and basting with melted herb butter after 1 hour and 30 minutes smoking.
10. When done, transfer the turkey breast to a cutting board, let it rest for 15 minutes, then carve it into pieces and serve.

Spatchcock Turkey

 Prep Time 15 min   **Cook Time** 5 hours   **Servings** 6

1 (18 pounds) turkey
2 tablespoons finely chopped fresh parsley
1 tablespoon finely chopped fresh rosemary
2 tablespoons finely chopped fresh thyme
1/2 cup melted butter
1 teaspoon garlic powder
1 teaspoon onion powder
1 teaspoon ground black pepper
2 teaspoons salt or to taste
2 tablespoons finely chopped scallions

1. Remove the turkey giblets and rinse the turkey, in and out, under cold running water.
2. Place the turkey on a working surface, breast side down. Use a poultry shear to cut the turkey along both sides of the backbone to remove the turkey backbone.
3. Flip the turkey over, backside down. Now, press the turkey down to flatten it.
4. In a mixing bowl, combine the parsley, rosemary, scallions, thyme, butter, pepper, salt, garlic, and onion powder.
5. Rub butter mixture over all sides of the turkey.
6. Preheat your griddle to high (450°F) with the lid closed for 15 minutes.
7. Place the turkey directly on the griddle grate and cook for 30 minutes. Reduce the heat to 300°F and cook for an additional 4 hours, or until the internal temperature of the thickest part of the thigh reaches 165°F. Take out the turkey meat from the griddle and let it rest for a few minutes. Cut into sizes and serve.

Nutrition: Calories: 480, Fat: 19 g, Carbs: 29 g, Protein: 54 g

Hoisin Turkey Wings

 Prep Time 20 min **Cook Time** 1 h 19 min **Servings** 8

2 pounds of turkey wings
1/2 cup hoisin sauce
1 tablespoon honey
2 teaspoons soy sauce
2 garlic cloves (minced)
1 teaspoon freshly grated ginger
2 teaspoons sesame oil
1 teaspoon pepper or to taste
1 teaspoons salt or to taste
1/4 cup pineapple juice
1 tablespoon chopped green onions
1 tablespoon sesame seeds
1 lemon (cut into wedges)

1. In a huge container, combine the honey, garlic, ginger, soy, hoisin sauce, sesame oil, pepper, and salt. Put all the mixture into a zip lock bag and add the wings. Refrigerate for 2 hours.
2. Remove turkey from the marinade and reserve the marinade. Let the turkey rest for a few minutes until it is at room temperature. Preheat your griddle to 300°F with the lid closed for 15 minutes.
3. Arrange the wings into a griddling basket and place the basket on the griddle.
4. Griddle for 1 hour or until the internal temperature of the wings reaches 165°F.
5. Meanwhile, pour the reserved marinade into a saucepan over medium-high heat. Stir in the pineapple juice. Wait to boil, then reduce heat and simmer until the sauce thickens. Brush the wings with sauce and cook for 6 minutes more. Remove the wings from heat. Serve and garnish it with green onions, sesame seeds, and lemon wedges.

Nutrition: Calories: 115, Fat: 4 g, Carbs: 12 g, Protein: 7 g

2 cups shredded cooked turkey
1 large sweet onion, sliced
8 slices of seedless rye
1/4 lb. thinly sliced Swiss cheese, about 8 slices
1/4 cup blue cheese dressing
1 cup mayonnaise
1 cup buffalo hot sauce
2 tablespoons unsalted butter
Blue cheese dressing

Buffalo Turkey Panini

 Prep Time 25 min **Cook Time** 1 hour **Servings** 8

1. Melt the butter in a large skillet on medium heat. Add the onions and cook for about 20 minutes.
2. Mix the buffalo sauce and mayonnaise in a medium bowl and toss with the chicken.
3. Put a slice of cheese on a piece of bread, then the turkey, and the onions, and top with another slice of cheese and another piece of bread. Repeat the process with the remaining sandwiches. Spread the butter on the top and bottom of the sandwich
4. Preheat the griddle to medium-high with the unit closed.
5. Cook the sandwiches for 4 minutes, and make sure to check halfway through. The bread should be brown, and the cheese should be melted. Serve the sandwiches with a side of the blue cheese dressing.

Nutrition: Calories: 387, Fat: 11.3 g, Protein: 9 g, Carbs: 7 g

Sweet Thai Cilantro Chili Turkey Quarters

 Prep Time 20 min   **Cook Time** 20 min   **Servings** 7

4 turkey n leg quarters, lightly coated with olive oil
1 cup and 1 teaspoon of water
¾ cup rice vinegar
1/2 cup white sugar
3 tablespoons freshly chopped cilantro
2 tablespoons freshly minced ginger root
2 teaspoons freshly minced garlic
2 tablespoons crushed red pepper flakes
2 tablespoons ketchup
2 tablespoons cornstarch
2 tablespoons fresh basil chiffonade ("chiffonade" is fancy for "thinly sliced")

1. Preparing the Ingredients
2. In a medium-sized saucepan, bring 1 cup of water and the vinegar to a boil over high heat.
3. Stir in sugar, cilantro, ginger, garlic, red pepper flakes, and ketchup; simmer for 5 Minutes.
4. In a small mixing bowl, mix 1 teaspoon warm water and 2 tablespoons cornstarch. Use a fork for mixing this, and what you'll end up with will resemble white school glue.
5. Slowly whisk the cornstarch mixture into the simmering sauce, and continue mixing until the sauce thickens. Set aside.
6. Bring the griddle to high heat. When the griddle is hot, place the turkey quarters skin side down and cook for 8 Minutes.
7. At 155°F internal temperature, glaze turkey with sauce and allow to finish cooking to an internal temperature of 165°F. Plate, garnish with basil, and serve.

Nutrition Calories: 513, Carbs: 8 g, Proteins: 37 g, Fat: 38 g

Curried Turkey Kebabs

 Prep Time 10 min   **Cook Time** 20 min   **Servings** 8

1. Add chicken in a large zip-lock bag.
2. In a small, bowl mix soy sauce, olive oil, curry powder, brown sugar, and peanut butter and pour over the chicken.
3. Seal bag and shake until turkey is well coated and place in the refrigerator overnight.
4. Thread marinated turkey onto skewers.
5. Preheat the griddle to high heat.
6. Spray griddle top with cooking spray.
7. Place turkey skewers onto the hot griddle top and cook for 12-15 minutes. Turn frequently.
8. Serve and enjoy.

1 1/2 lbs. turkey breasts, boneless and cut into 1-inch pieces
1/2 cup soy sauce
1 tablespoon olive oil
1 tablespoon curry powder
1 tablespoon brown sugar
2 tablespoons peanut butter

Nutrition: Calories: 430, Fat: 20 g, Carbs: 7 g, Protein: 53 g

Tailgate Young Turkey

Prep Time 35 min **Cook Time** 4 hours **Servings** 7

1 fresh or thawed frozen young turkey
6 glasses of extra virgin olive oil with roasted garlic flavor
6 original Yang dry lab or poultry seasonings

1. Remove excess Fat: and skin from turkey breasts and cavities.
2. Slowly separate the skin of the turkey to its breast and a quarter of the leg, leaving the skin intact.
3. Apply olive oil to the chest, under the skin, and on the skin.
4. Gently rub or season to the chest cavity, under the skin, and on the skin.
5. Preheat the griddle to 225°F.
6. Put the turkey meat on the griddle with the chest up.
7. Cook the turkey for 4 hours at 225°F until the thickest part of the turkey's chest reaches an internal temperature of 170°F, and the juice is clear.
8. Before engraving, place the turkey under a loose foil tent for 20 minutes

Nutrition: Calories: 240, Carbs: 27 g, Fat: 9 g, Protein: 15 g

---

Thanksgiving Dinner Turkey

Prep Time 20 min **Cook Time** 3 h 25 min **Servings** 8

1/2 lb. butter, softened
2 tablespoons fresh thyme, chopped
2 tablespoons fresh rosemary, chopped
6 garlic cloves, crushed
1 (20-lb.) whole turkey, neck, and giblets removed
Salt and ground black pepper

1. Set the griddle temperature to 300°F and preheat with a closed lid for 15 mins, using charcoal.
2. In a bowl, place butter, fresh herbs, garlic, salt, and black pepper and mix well.
3. Separate the turkey skin from the breast to create a pocket.
4. Stuff the breast pocket with a 1/4-inch thick layer of the butter mixture.
5. Season turkey with salt and black pepper.
6. Arrange the turkey onto the griddle and cook for 3 hours.
7. Remove the turkey from the griddle and place it on a cutting board for about 15-20 minutes before carving.
8. Cut the turkey into desired-sized pieces and serve.

Nutrition: Calories: 965, Carbs: 1 g, Protein: 106 g, Fat: 52 g

---

BBQ Pulled Turkey Sandwiches

Prep Time 25 min **Cook Time** 40 min **Servings** 6

6 skin-on turkey thighs
6 split and buttered buns
1 1/2 cups of chicken broth
1 cup of BBQ sauce
Poultry rub

1. Season the turkey thighs on both sides with a poultry rub.
2. Set the griddle to preheat by pushing the temperature to 180°F.
3. Place the turkey elements on the griddle.
4. Now transfer the thighs to an aluminum foil, which is disposable, and then pour the brine right around the thighs.
5. Cover it with a lid. Now increase the griddle temperature to 325°F and roast the thigh till the internal temperature reaches 180°F.
6. Remove the foil from the griddle but do not turn off the griddle.
7. Let the turkey thighs cool down a little.
8. Now pour the dripping and serve.
9. Remove the skin and discard it.
10. Pull the meat into shreds and return it to the foil.
11. Add 1 more cup of BBQ sauce and some more dripping.
12. Now cover the foil with a lid and re-heat the turkey on the griddle for half an hour.
13. Serve and enjoy.

Nutrition: Calories: 178, Fat: 1 g, Carbs: 47 g, Protein: 2 g

Roast Turkey Orange

 Prep Time 25 min **Cook Time** 2 hours **Servings** 7

1 frozen long island turkey
3 tablespoons west
1 large orange, cut into wedges
3 celery stems chopped into large chunks
half a small red onion, a quarter
Orange sauce:
2 orange cups
2 tablespoons soy sauce
2 tablespoons orange marmalade
2 tablespoons honey
3 teaspoons grated raw

1. Remove the nibble from the turkey's cavity and neck and retain or discard it for another use. Wash the duck and pat some dry paper towels.
2. Remove excess Fat: from the tail, neck, and cavity. Use a sharp scalpel knife tip to pierce the turkey's skin entirely so that it does not penetrate the duck's meat, to help dissolve the Fat: layer beneath the skin.
3. Add the seasoning inside the cavity with one cup of rub or seasoning.
4. Season the outside of the turkey with the remaining friction or seasoning.
5. Fill the cavity with orange wedges, celery, and onion. Duck legs are tied with butcher twine to make filling easier. Place the turkey's breast up on a small rack of shallow roast bread.
6. To make the sauce, mix the ingredients in the saucepan over low heat and cook until the sauce is thick and syrupy. Set aside and let cool.
7. Preheat the griddle to 350°F.
8. Roast the turkey at 350°F for 2 hours.
9. After 2 hours, brush the turkey freely with orange sauce.
10. Roast the orange glass turkey for another 30 minutes, making sure that the inside temperature of the thickest part of the leg reaches 165°F.
11. Place turkey under a loose foil tent for 20 minutes before serving.
12. Discard the orange wedge, celery, and onion. Serve with a quarter of turkey with poultry scissors.

Nutrition: Calories: 216, Carbs: 2 g, Fat: 11 g, Protein: 34 g

---

Thanksgiving Turkey

 Prep Time 20 min **Cook Time** 4 h 15 min **Servings** 6

1. In a mixing bowl, combine the butter, sage, rosemary, 1 teaspoon black pepper, 1 teaspoon salt, thyme, parsley, and garlic.
2. Use your fingers to loosen the skin from the turkey.
3. Generously rub the butter mixture under the turkey skin and all over the turkey as well.
4. Season turkey generously with herb mix.
5. Preheat the griddle to 300°F with the lid closed for 15 minutes.
6. Place the turkey on the griddle and roast for about 4 hours, or until the turkey thigh temperature reaches 160°F.
7. Take out the turkey meat from the griddle and let it rest for a few minutes. Cut into sizes and serve.

2 cups butter (softened)
1 tablespoon cracked black pepper
2 teaspoons kosher salt
2 tablespoons freshly chopped rosemary
2 tablespoons freshly chopped parsley
2 tablespoons freshly chopped sage
2 teaspoons dried thyme
6 garlic cloves (minced)
1 (18 pounds) turkey

Nutrition: Calories: 278, Fat: 30 g, Carbs: 1 g, Protein: 13 g

Pork Recipes

Griddled Stuff Pork Chops

 Prep Time 15 min   **Cook Time** 10 min   **Servings** 4

1. Cut a slit on the meaty side of the pork chops to create a pocket. Set aside.
2. In a bowl, mix the spinach, parmesan cheese, shallot, thyme, and paprika. Mix until well combined.
3. Stuff the pork with the spinach mixture. Secure the ends with a toothpick.
4. Season the pork with salt and pepper.
5. Heat the griddle to medium and brush with oil.
6. Place the pork chops and cook each side for 9 minutes.

4 thick-cut pork chops
10 ounces chopped spinach, blanched
4 ounces grated parmesan cheese
1 shallot, chopped
1 tablespoon dried thyme
1 tablespoon paprika

Nutrition: Calories: 467, Protein: 47 g, Carbs: 11 g, Fat: 11 g

Mustard and Rosemary Pork Chops

 Prep Time 15 min   **Cook Time** 11 min   **Servings** 1

2 tablespoons mild mustard
3 tablespoons olive oil
1 Fat: garlic clove, sliced
2 sprigs rosemary, chopped
1 tablespoon sherry or balsamic vinegar
4 pork shoulder

1. In a bowl, mix the mustard, olive oil, garlic, rosemary, and balsamic vinegar.
2. Brush the pork with the seasoning mixture.
3. Heat the griddle to medium and brush with oil.
4. Cook the pork for 7 to 9 minutes on each side.
5.

Nutrition: Calories: 506, Protein: 42 g, Carbs: 2 g, Fat: 37 g

Simple And Easy Griddled Pork Chops

2 pork chops
2 tablespoons olive oil
Salt and pepper to taste
1 teaspoon smoked paprika

1. Preheat the griddle pan to high and brush with oil.
2. Cook the pork for 5 minutes on each side.
3. Check for the internal temperature and make sure that it reaches 145°F.

Nutrition: Calories: 391, Protein: 40 g, Carbs: 1 g, Fat: 14 g

---

Pork And Peaches

Prep Time 10 min   Cook Time 14 min   Servings 3

2 lbs. Boneless pork butt
8 tablespoons extra virgin olive oil
10 cloves of garlic, minced
2 tablespoons rosemary leaves, chopped
Salt and pepper to taste
6 fresh peaches, halved and pitted
4 tablespoons unsalted butter, cubed

1. Heat the griddle pan to medium and brush with oil.
2. Score the pork butt with a knife. Rub the meat with oil. Season the pork with garlic, rosemary leaves, and salt
3. Place on one side of the griddle and cover with foil on top. Cook for 7 minutes on each side.
4. Place the sliced peaches next to the pork and cook until golden, then throw in the butter. Once done, set aside.
5. Allow the pork to rest before slicing.
6. Serve pork slices with griddled peaches.

Nutrition: Calories: 688, Protein: 35 g, Carbs: 85 g, Fat: 27 g

---

Pulled Pork Griddle Cakes

Prep Time 15 min   Cook Time 20 min   Servings 2

11/2cup self-rising white cornmeal mix
1/2cup all-purpose flour
1 tablespoon sugar
1 2/3 cup buttermilk
3 tablespoons butter, melted
2 large eggs, beaten
2 cups leftover pulled pork

1. Heat the griddle pan over medium heat and brush the pan with oil.
2. Mix all ingredients in a bowl and mix until well combined.
3. Pour1/2cup batter on the griddle pot and cook for 3 minutes on each side.
4. Repeat until all batter is cooked.

Nutrition: Calories: 250, Protein: 14 g, Carbs: 29 g, Fat: 8 g

---

Easy Griddled Pork Chops

2 center-cut boneless pork chops
2 teaspoons extra virgin olive oil
Salt and pepper to taste

1. Brush pork chops with oil and season with salt and pepper to taste.
2. Heat the griddle pan and brush the pan with oil.
3. Cook for 5 minutes on each side.
4. Remove the pork chops and let them rest for 5 minutes.

Nutrition: Calories: 253, Protein: 40 g, Carbs: 2 g, Fat: 9 g

Honey-Mustard Marinated Pork Chops

Prep Time 15 min | Cook Time 10 min | Servings 4

2 center-cut pork chops
1 teaspoon wet mustard
1 teaspoon honey
1 teaspoon soy sauce
1/2tsp ground pepper
2 dashes of Worcestershire sauce

1. Marinate the pork chops with mustard, honey, soy sauce, ground pepper, and Worcestershire sauce.
2. Marinate for 6 hours in the fridge.
3. Heat the griddle pan to medium and brush with oil.
4. Cook the pork chops for 5 minutes on each side.
5. Allow resting before slicing.

Nutrition: Calories: 251, Protein: 40 g, Carbs: 5 g, Fat: 7 g

Tandoori Pork

 Prep Time 10 min | Cook Time 10 min | Servings 5

1. Place all ingredients in a bowl and mix until the pork loin is coated with the seasoning. Marinate in the fridge for at least 12 hours.
2. Heat the griddle pan over medium heat and brush with oil.
3. Cook the pork chops for 5 minutes on each side.
4. Serve the meat with naan bread, yogurt, and sliced cucumbers.

4 14-ounce pork loin
4-inch ginger, grated
12 cloves of garlic, minced
1 tablespoon ground cumin
1 tablespoon ground coriander
1 tablespoon paprika
21/2tsp garam masala
1 teaspoon ground fenugreek seeds
2 teaspoons Indian chili paste
5 tablespoons lemon juice

Nutrition: Calories: 845, Protein: 112 g, Carbs: 7 g, Fat: 38 g

Griddled Pork Brisket

 Prep Time 10 min | Cook Time 30 min | Servings 6

2.5 lbs. pork brisket, sliced to 1-inch thick
¾ cup pork seasoning

1. Season the pork with the seasonings.
2. Heat the griddle pan to medium heat and brush with oil.
3. Cook on all sides for 10 to 15 minutes while stirring constantly.

Nutrition: Calories: 247, Protein: 27 g, Carbs: 0 g, Fat: 8 g

Griddle-Roasted Pork Chop

 Prep Time 15 min **Cook Time** 10 min **Servings** 3

3 lbs. Pork chops
1 tablespoon cumin seeds, ground
1 tablespoon dill seeds, ground
1 teaspoon ground cinnamon
1 teaspoon ground black pepper
1 teaspoon salt
1/8 teaspoon dried chili flakes

1. Heat the griddle pan to medium heat and brush with oil.
2. Season the pork chops with the rest of the ingredients.
3. Place the pork chops on the griddle pan and cook for 5 minutes on each side.
4. Allow resting before slicing.

Nutrition: Calories: 484, Protein: 59 g, Carbs: 2 g, Fat: 26 g

Pork Chops with Lemon and Oregano

 Prep Time 10 min **Cook Time** 20 min **Servings** 2

1. In a bowl, mix the olive oil, lemon juice, oregano, salt, and pepper. Mix until well combined.
2. Brush the spice rub all over the pork chops.
3. Heat the griddle pan to medium heat and brush with oil.
4. Cook for 5 minutes on each side.

2 tablespoons olive oil
4 tablespoons lemon juice
2 teaspoons dried oregano
Salt and pepper to taste
4 pork chops

Nutrition: Calories: 337, Protein: 29 g, Carbs: 2 g, Fat: 23 g

Griddle Pan Liempo

 Prep Time 10 min **Cook Time** 10 min **Servings** 1

3 lbs. Pork belly
1/2cup soy sauce
Juice from 1 lemon
1 tablespoon minced garlic
1/2cup ketchup
1/4tsp black pepper

1. Combine all ingredients in a bowl and mix well.
2. Heat the griddle pan to high and brush with oil.
3. Cook the pork for 8 to 10 minutes on each side.
4. Serve with pickles.

Nutrition: Calories: 360, Protein: 41 g, Carbs: 15 g, Fat: 16 g

Breaded Pork Chops

 Prep Time 20 min   **Cook Time** 20 min   **Servings** 6

2 tablespoons apple cider vinegar
1 tablespoon brown sugar
2 tablespoons butter
1/8 teaspoons cayenne pepper
2 eggs, beaten
1/2 cup flour
1/2 tablespoons horseradish
1/2 lemon, juiced
1/2 cup mayonnaise
1 1/2 cup panko breadcrumbs
6 pork chops, bone-in
1 tablespoon sea salt
1/4 cup sour cream
1/2 tablespoons mustard (stone ground)
1/2 cup vegetable oil

Nutrition: Calories: 356, Fat: 19 g, Carbs: 17 g, Protein: 24 g

1. Place the pork chops on even a sheet tray and pat dry with a paper towel before seasoning with Smoked Hickory and Honey Sea Salt.
2. In three separate bowls, combine beaten egg, flour, and bread crumbs. Set aside each pork chop after dipping it in flour, beaten egg, and breadcrumbs.
3. Make the White Sauce as follows: Mayonnaise, apple cider vinegar, sour cream, brown sugar, horseradish, spicy brown mustard, lemon juice, and cayenne pepper should all be whisked together in a small bowl. Set aside after whisking until fully blended.
4. Set the griddle to medium heat and fire it up. Then pour in the oil. When the oil starts to smoke, add butter and melt before putting out the pork chops. Cook the pork chops for two to three minutes on each side, or till golden brown and crisp 1 minute per side for thicker chops.
5. Serve the breaded pork chops with White Sauce while they're still warm.

Griddle Pork Skewers

 Prep Time 5 min   **Cook Time** 10 min   **Servings** 7

1. Place the pork in a bowl and pour in beer, garlic, salt, pepper, and thyme.
2. Marinate inside the fridge for at least 6 hours.
3. Skewer the marinated pork cubes with onion wedges.
4. Heat the griddle pan to medium and brush with oil.
5. Cook the skewered pork for 5 minutes on each side.

2 lbs. Boneless pork shoulder, cut into cubes
1/4 cup beer
3 cloves garlic, minced
Salt and pepper to taste
8 sprigs of thyme leaves
1 large onion, cut into wedges

Nutrition: Calories: 423, Protein: 27 g, Carbs: 3 g, Fat: 21 g

Griddle Pork Fried Rice

Prep Time 10 min   **Cook Time** 10 min   **Servings** 4

4 tablespoons oil
1 small onion, chopped
1 cup sliced pork
1 cup frozen peas
3 cups leftover rice, chilled
2 eggs, beaten
1/8 cup soy sauce
1 teaspoon sesame oil
Chopped scallions

1. Heat the griddle pan to high and brush with oil.
2. Sauté the onion for 1 minute before adding the pork. Stir for 5 minutes until the pork is lightly golden.
3. Stir in the peas and rice. Mix until well-combined.
4. Create a well in the middle of the rice mixture and add the eggs.
5. Stir to combine.
6. Season with soy sauce and sesame oil.
7. Mix for another 3 minutes.
8. Garnish with scallions before serving.

Nutrition: Calories: 152, Protein: 6 g, Carbs: 17 g, Fat: 152 g

Japanese Griddled Pork Chops

Prep Time 20 min   **Cook Time** 20 min   **Servings** 2

1/3 cup low-sodium soy sauce
1 tablespoon rice vinegar
1 tablespoon honey
2 teaspoons toasted sesame oil
1/4tsp red pepper flakes
2 bone-in pork loin chops
Black and white sesame seeds
Sliced scallions

1. Place all ingredients in a bowl and marinate in the fridge for at least 12 hours.
2. Heat the griddle pan to medium and brush with oil.
3. Cook for 5 to 8 minutes on each side.
4. Garnish with toasted sesame seeds and scallions.

Nutrition: Calories: 430, Protein: 44 g, Carbs: 12 g, Fat: 22 g

Spicy Griddled Pork Chops

Prep Time 5 min   **Cook Time** 20 min   **Servings** 4

1-quart lukewarm water
1/4 cup salt
1/4 cup sugar
4 boneless loin pork chops,1-inch thick
2 tablespoons sweet paprika
1 tablespoon smoky paprika
1 teaspoon garlic powder
1 teaspoon dry mustard
Salt and pepper to taste

1. Place the water, 1/4 cup salt, and sugar in a deep bowl. Dissolve the salt and sugar before adding the pork.
2. Place in the fridge for 24 hours and allow to marinate in the brine.
3. After 24 hours, remove pork from the brine and pat dry.
4. Rub the pork with the remaining spices and seasonings.
5. Heat the griddle pan to medium and brush with oil.
6. Cook for 5 to 8 minutes on each side.

Nutrition: Calories: 280, Protein: 30 g, Carbs: 16 g, Fat: 4 g

Pulled pork griddled cheese

 Prep Time 5 min   **Cook Time** 5 min   **Servings** 2

2 slices of Cheddar Cheese
2 oz. Pulled Pork
1 tablespoon butter
1 tablespoon BBQ sauce

1. Butter one slice of bread first.
2. Turn one of the bread slices over so that the butter side is on the bottom, or the unbuttered side remains facing up.
3. Top the bread with a layer of shredded Cheddar cheese.
4. After that, cover the cheese with a layer of pulled pork.
5. Add a dash of your preferred BBQ sauce to the pulled pork.
6. Finally, put the second slice of bread on top of the buttered side of the BBQ pulled pork. Cook for about two minutes on each side on a griddle pan over medium-low heat till browned from both sides

Nutrition: Calories: 495, Fat: 25 g, Carbs: 47 g, Protein: 19 g

Garlic Butter Pork Chops

 Prep Time 5 min   **Cook Time** 15 min   **Servings** 1

1 package of pork chops
1 teaspoon salt
1/2 teaspoons black pepper
1 teaspoon garlic, minced
8 tablespoons butter
1/4 cup fresh herbs (oregano, parsley, and mint)

1. Combine the butter, black pepper, salt, and chopped herbs in a small mixing bowl. Then, on top of the pork, sprinkle the sauce.
2. Preheat the griddle to medium-high. After that, place the pork on the griddle to sear it quickly. The cook time will be determined by the thickness of your chops and the temperature you wish to cook. Per side, it took me approximately 3-5 minutes.
3. Allow the pork chops to rest for 5-10 minutes before serving.
4. Serve and have a good time.

Nutrition: Calories: 290, Fat: 29 g, Carbs: 1 g, Protein: 0 g

Glazed Pork Chops

 Prep Time 5 min   **Cook Time** 10 min   **Servings** 4

4 pork loin chops, bone-in
1/3 cup cider vinegar plus 1 tablespoon, divided
3 tablespoons soy sauce
3 garlic cloves, minced
1 1/2 teaspoons cornstarch

Nutrition: Calories: 224, Fat: 8 g, Carbs: 2 g, Protein: 32 g

1. Brown pork chops in a griddle pan over medium heat for about two minutes per side. Combine soy sauce, 1/3 cup vinegar, and garlic in a mixing bowl; pour over pork chops. Bring the water to a boil. Reduce heat to low and cook, covered, for 7-9 minutes, until a thermometer placed in the pork reaches 145°F.
2. Stir together the cornstarch and the remaining vinegar until smooth, then pour into the pan. Bring to a boil, then cook and stir for 1 minute, or until sauce has thickened

Simple Griddled Pork Chops with "Secret" Sweet Rub

Prep Time 10 min   **Cook Time** 30 min   **Servings** 4

4 pork loin chops
For Secret sweet BBQ rub
2 tablespoons brown sugar
2 teaspoons kosher salt
1 teaspoon black pepper, cracked
1 teaspoon paprika
1/2 teaspoons mustard, ground
1/2 teaspoons cayenne pepper

1. In a small bowl, combine all of the rub ingredients and set aside.
2. Allow 10 minutes for the griddle to heat up to medium-high.
3. Pour the rub into the pork loin chops.
4. Cook the chops on each side for 3-4 minutes on the griddle.
5. Remove the pork chops off the direct heat and continue to cook for another 5-6 minutes per side, or until internal temperature reaches 145°F.
6. Allow the chops to cool for 5-6 mins before slicing.

Nutrition: Calories: 149, Fat: 8 g, Carbs: 21 g, Protein: 1 g

Sage Pork Chops with Cider Pan Gravy

Prep Time 5 min   **Cook Time** 10 min   **Servings** 2

4 6-ounces each pork loin chops, bone-in, and center-cut
1/2 teaspoons salt
1/4 teaspoons pepper
3 tablespoons sage leaves, dried
1/4 cup all-purpose flour
2 tablespoons butter
2 tablespoons canola oil
1/2 cup chicken broth (reduced sodium)
1/2 cup apple cider vinegar
1/4 cup whipping cream, heavy
Fresh parsley, minced

1. Season the chops with pepper and salt, and sage. To lightly coat, dip in flour.
2. Brown chops on all sides in a griddle pan with oil and butter over medium heat. Remove the pan from the heat.
3. Bring cider and broth to a boil in the pan, stirring to dislodge browned pieces from the bottom. Cook, constantly stirring, until the cream has thickened. Reduce to a medium heat setting. Cook, covered, for 5-7 minutes, until a thermometer placed in the pork reads 145°F. Allow it cool for a few minutes before garnishing with parsley.

Nutrition: Calories: 449, Fat: 32 g, Carbs: 10 g, Protein: 29 g

Apple's 'n' Onion Topped Chops

Prep Time 20 min   **Cook Time** 15 min   **Servings** 4

4 teaspoons canola oil, divided
4 pork loin chops, boneless
3 cups slices of sweet onion
2 medium apples, peeled and sliced
1/2 cup water
2 tablespoons brown sugar
1 tablespoon cider vinegar
1 teaspoon garlic powder
1/2 teaspoons salt
1/2 teaspoons pepper
1/4 teaspoons rosemary, crushed and dried

1. Cook chops till browned, about three minutes on each side, in a griddle pan with 2 tablespoons of canola oil at medium-high heat. Remove the meat and keep it warm by setting it aside.
2. In the same pan, sauté and toss the onion for Seven minutes or till golden brown, using the remaining 2 tablespoons of canola oil. Cook for another 3 minutes, stirring occasionally.
3. Water, vinegar, brown sugar, garlic powder, pepper, salt, and rosemary should all be mixed in a bowl. Add the mixture to your pork chops and include the apples as well. Reduce the heat to low, cover, and simmer for 6-8 minutes, or until the apples are crisp-tender and a thermometer placed in the pork reads 145°F. Before serving, set aside for 5 minutes.

Nutrition: Calories: 178, Fat: 1 g, Carbs: 47 g, Protein: 2 g

Garlic soy pork chops

 Prep Time 15 min **Cook Time** 35 min **Servings** 5

1. Mix chopped fresh garlic, soy sauce, olive oil, salt, black pepper, and garlic powder in a small mixing bowl. Fill a freezer bag halfway with the mixture and chops and seal it tightly, massaging everything to blend. Refrigerate for 30 minutes to 6 hours after marinating.
2. Remove pork chops from the freezer bag and place them on the counter for 22-25 minutes to reach room temperature.
3. Preheat the Griddle to medium-high heat. Add a drizzle of olive oil (approximately 12 tablespoons) and 1 1/2 tablespoons butter, mixing it in with the oil. Place the chops on the griddle one at a time. Allow cooking for 4-5 minutes before flipping and seasoning with cracked black pepper. Cook for 3-4 minutes after flipping and spreading 1.5 tablespoons of butter underneath the chops.
4. Over and all around the chops, drizzle a dash of soy sauce (about 2 tablespoons). Cook for another 2-4 minutes, then lower to medium-low heat and flip 2-3 more times till chops are fully done.
5. Place the chops on top of 1 tablespoon of softened butter in a mixing bowl. Allow 10 minutes to rest before cutting into them. Serve with chopped parsley on top.

5 pork chops, thick-cut
4 garlic cloves
1/2 cup olive oil (extra virgin)
1/2 cup soy sauce (low sodium)
1/2 teaspoons garlic powder
1/2 teaspoons sea salt
1 teaspoon black pepper, fresh cracked
1/2 cup curly parsley
1/2 stick of real butter
Olive oil (extra virgin) for griddle top

Nutrition: Calories: 178, Fat: 7 g, Carbs: 1 g, Protein: 25 g

83

Balsamic Pork Chops

 Prep Time 15 min **Cook Time** 20 min **Servings** 4

1. Balsamic vinegar, soy sauce, Worcestershire sauce, oil, black pepper, garlic, and cayenne pepper are whisked together.
2. Put pork chops in a big resealable bag and cover with marinade.
3. Refrigerate for 3 to 4 hours.
4. 15 minutes before cooking, take out pork chops from the fridge.
5. Preheat the griddle to high and brush it with a thin layer of olive oil.
6. Cook pork chops on the griddle for 3-4 minutes per side, or till the internal temperature hits 145°F.

1/3 cup balsamic vinegar
1/3 cup Worcestershire sauce
1/4 cup soy sauce (reduced-sodium)
2 tablespoons olive oil
2 minced garlic cloves
1/2 teaspoons black pepper
1/4 teaspoons cayenne pepper
4 pork chops, bone-in

Nutrition: Calories: 310, Fat: 10 g, Carbs: 23 g, Protein: 31 g

Pork Cutlets

Prep Time	Cook Time	Servings
10 min	10 min	7

1 lb. pork cutlets, thinly sliced
1 cup breadcrumbs (Italian seasoned)
1/2 cup cheese (Pecorino Romano)
1 teaspoon thyme
2 eggs
1/4 cup milk
1 teaspoon garlic powder
Salt and pepper, to taste
1 tbsp Vegetable oil

Nutrition: Calories: 139, Fat: 5 g, Carbs: 0 g, Protein: 25 g

1. Combine cheese, breadcrumbs, and thyme in one of two separate shallow bowls. In a separate bowl, whisk together garlic powder, eggs, milk, salt, and black pepper.
2. Dip one cutlet at a time in egg wash, then breadcrumbs, and set aside on a plate until all of the cutlets are evenly coated.
3. Preheat the Griddle to 350°F, medium-low heat.
4. With a spray bottle, drizzle oil into a place the size of the cutlet, then dip it into the oil. Rep with each cutlet. Cook for approximately 2-3 minutes, until it is golden brown.
5. Drizzle oil over the cutlet before flipping and cooking for another 2-3 minutes, or until golden brown. Lift the cutlet with tongs or a spatula and spray a little additional oil beneath.
6. Sprinkle with sea salt and pecorino cheese and place on a cooling rack.

Raspberry Pork Medallions

Prep Time	Cook Time	Servings
15 min	20 min	6

1 lb. pork tenderloin
1 tablespoon canola oil
2 tablespoons soy sauce (reduced sodium)
1 garlic clove, minced
1/2 teaspoons ginger, ground
1 cup raspberries, fresh
2 tablespoons raspberry fruit, seedless
2 teaspoons fresh basil, minced
1/2 teaspoons mint, minced and fresh

1. Slice tenderloin crosswise into 8 pieces and pound each to 1/2-inch thickness with a meat mallet. Heat the oil in a griddle pan over medium-high heat. Cook for 4-5 minutes on each side till a thermometer reaches 145°F on both sides. Remove from the pan and set aside to keep heated.
2. Lower heat to medium-low and mix in garlic, soy sauce, and ginger to loosen browned pieces from the bottom of the pan. Cook and whisk for 2-3 minutes, or until slightly thickened, adding raspberries, basil, spreadable fruit, and, if desired, mint.

Nutrition: Calories: 206, Fat: 8 g, Carbs: 10 g, Protein: 24 g

Pork Chops with Parmesan Sauce

Prep Time	Cook Time	Servings
15 min	10 min	4

4 pork loin chops, boneless
1/2 teaspoon salt
1/4 teaspoon pepper
1 tablespoon butter
2 tablespoons flour (all-purpose)
1 cup milk (fat-free)
1/3 cup parmesan cheese, grated
2 tablespoon onion, grated
3 teaspoons parsley, minced and fresh
1/4 teaspoon thyme, dried
1/4 teaspoon nutmeg, ground

1. Season pork chops with pepper and salt. Cook chops in butter in a griddle pan over medium heat till meat juices run clear; transfer and keep warm.
2. Stir together the milk and flour until smooth, then pour into the pan. Bring to a boil, reduce to low heat, and cook, constantly stirring, for 2 minutes, or until the sauce has thickened. Stir in the remaining ingredients and heat until hot.

Nutrition: Calories: 244, Fat: 11 g, Carbs: 7 g, Protein: 27 g

Garden Pork Stir-Fry

 Prep Time
5 min

 Cook Time
10 min

 Servings
6

1. Stir-fry the pork in a griddle pan with cooking spray until it is no longer pink, around 5 min. Stir-fry for 3 minutes, or until crisp-tender, with the zucchini, onion, mushrooms, and green pepper.

2. Mix the soy sauce, cornstarch, water, and garlic powder in a small bowl and whisk until smooth.

3. Toss everything into the griddle. Reduce to low heat and cook, constantly stirring, for 1-2 minutes, or until the sauce has thickened. Serve with a side of rice.

1 lb. pork loin, boneless, sliced into ¾-inch cubes
2 cups julienned zucchini
1/2 lb. mushrooms, sliced and fresh
1 medium onion, sliced into wedges
1 cup green pepper (julienned)
1 tablespoon cornstarch
3 tablespoons soy sauce (reduced sodium)
1 tablespoon cold water
1/4 teaspoons garlic powder
Cooked rice, hot

Nutrition: Calories: 196, Fat: 6 g, Carbs: 10 g, Protein: 25 g

Basil Pork Chops

 Prep Time
10 min

 Cook Time
10 min

 Servings
4

1. Combine the first four ingredients in a mixing bowl; gradually add 1 tablespoon of oil. Rub the pork chops on all sides.

2. Cook chops in remaining oil in a griddle pan over medium heat till a thermometer reads 145°F, 4-5 minutes per side. Allow for 5 minutes of cooking time before serving.

1/4 cup brown sugar, packed
1 1/2 teaspoons basil, dried
1/2 teaspoons salt
1/2 teaspoons chili powder
2 tablespoons canola oil, divided
4 pork loin chops, boneless

Nutrition: Calories: 152, Fat: 8 g, Carbs: 14 g, Protein: 6 g

Beef Recipes

Teppanyaki Beef with Vegetables

 Prep Time 5 min   **Cook Time** 10 min   **Servings** 2

1. Season the steak with salt, pepper, and garlic powder.
2. Set your griddle to high heat on one side and medium-high heat on the other side.
3. Add some vegetable oil to the medium-hot side and add the onion rings, zucchini, and snap peas. Season with a little salt and pepper.
4. Add the steaks to the hot side and cook for 3 minutes. Flip, top with butter, and add soy sauce to the steaks. Continue cooking for additional 4 minutes.
5. Remove the steak and vegetables from the griddle and slice the steak across the grain before serving.

Steak:
2- 1 lb. sirloin steaks
1 tablespoon garlic powder
4 tablespoons soy sauce
1 white onion, sliced into large rounds
3 zucchinis, sliced into 1/4 inch thick flats
2 cups snap peas
4 tablespoons vegetable oil
3 tablespoons butter
Salt and black pepper

Nutrition: Calories: 484, Fat: 24 g, Carbs: 14 g, Protein: 51 g

Rib-Eye Steak with Herbed Steak Butter

 Prep Time 156 min   **Cook Time** 55 min   **Servings** 2

1 (24-ounce) bone-in Tomahawk rib-eye, about 2 1/2 inches thick
Olive oil
Sea salt
Fresh cracked pepper
3 tablespoons premium French butter
1/2 teaspoon Herbes de Provence

1. Beat butter with herbs in a small mixing bowl, cover, and refrigerate until ready to cook the rib-eye.
2. Rub the rib-eye liberally with olive oil, salt, and pepper until the entire steak is covered.
3. Wrap lightly with cling wrap and place in the refrigerator to marinate for 12 hours.
4. Preheat the griddle to high heat on one side and medium-low on the other side, at least one hour before cooking.
5. Remove the steak from the refrigerator and leave it at room temperature during the hour that the griddle is preheating.
6. Place the steak on the center of the hottest side of the griddle. Do this for both sides for about 10 minutes.
7. Move the rib-eye to the cooler side of the griddle and cook to rare, about 25 to 30 minutes.
8. Transfer rib-eye to the griddle, add herbed butter on top, and lightly tent it with tin foil to rest for at least 15 minutes before carving.
9. Serve with your favorite sides!

Nutrition: Calories: 549, Fat: 40 g, Carbs: 3 g, Protein: 41 g

Basic Juicy NY Strip Steak

 Prep Time **Cook Time** **Servings**
10 min   15 min   1

1 (8 ounces) NY strip steak
1 tsp Olive oil
Sea salt
Fresh ground black pepper

1. Remove the steak from the refrigerator and let it come to room temperature, about 30 to 45 minutes.
2. Preheat the griddle to medium-high heat and brush with olive oil.
3. Season the steak on all sides with salt and pepper.
4. Cook steak for about 4 to 5 minutes.
5. Flip and cook about 4 minutes more for medium rare steak; between 125°F and 130°F on a meat thermometer.
6. Transfer the steak to a plate and let it rest for 5 minutes before serving.

Nutrition: Calories: 980, Fat: 86 g, Carbs: 0 g, Protein: 184 g

---

High-Low Strip Steak

 Prep Time **Cook Time** **Servings**
5 min   15 min   2

2 (1-pound) New York strip steaks, trimmed
For the rub:
1 bunch of thyme sprigs
1 bunch of rosemary sprigs
1 bunch of sage sprigs
1 1/2 teaspoons black pepper, divided
3/4 teaspoon sea salt, divided
1/2 teaspoon garlic powder
2 tablespoons chopped fresh flat-leaf parsley
2 tablespoons extra-virgin olive oil

1. Preheat the griddle to high heat.
2. Combine rub ingredients in a small mixing bowl and rub steaks with spice mixture; let rest for 10 minutes.
3. Place steaks on the griddle and cook for 1 minute per side.
4. Turn the griddle down to medium heat.
5. Turn steaks and cook for 3 additional minutes per side; or until the thermometer registers 135°F for medium rare.
6. Remove steaks to a platter.
7. Let rest for 5 minutes. Cut steaks across the grain into thin slices.

Nutrition: Calories: 347, Fat: 20 g, Carbs: 4 g, Protein: 39 g

---

Tuscan-Style Steak with Crispy Potatoes

2 bone-in porterhouse steaks
1 1/2 lb. small potatoes, like Yukon Gold, scrubbed but skins left on, halved
4 tablespoons extra-virgin olive oil, divided
Sea salt and freshly ground pepper, to taste
2 teaspoons red wine, like Sangiovese or Montepulciano
1 teaspoon balsamic vinegar
Pinch red pepper flakes
3 fresh rosemary sprigs, needles removed (discard stems)

 Prep Time **Cook Time** **Servings**
5 min   22 min   3

1. Add potatoes to a large pot and cover with water, bring to a boil over high heat, then reduce the heat to medium-high and cook until the potatoes are almost tender about 10 minutes. Drain, add to a medium mixing bowl, coat with 2 tablespoons olive oil, and set aside.
2. Preheat the griddle to medium heat.
3. Whisk 2 tablespoons olive oil, rosemary, red wine, vinegar, and pepper flakes; add steaks to marinade and set aside until ready to cook.
4. Sprinkle potatoes with salt and pepper.
5. Add steaks to one side of the griddle and potatoes to the other.
6. Cook the steak for 5 minutes, flip it, and 4 minutes on the other side for medium rare.
7. Add the potatoes to cook for 5 minutes.
8. Transfer steaks to a cutting board and tent with aluminum foil and let rest for 5 minutes while potatoes are cooking.
9. Divide each steak into 2 pieces and divide among 4 dinner plates. Spoon some potatoes around the steak and serve hot!

Nutrition: Calories: 366, Fat: 23 g, Carbs: 27 g, Protein: 13 g

Caprese Griddled Filet Mignon

 Prep Time 15 min   **Cook Time** 12 min   **Servings** 7

1. Lightly brush each filet, on all sides, with olive oil and rub with garlic salt.
2. Preheat the griddle to high. Place steaks on the griddle, reduce heat to medium, tent with foil, and cook for 5 minutes.
3. Flip, re-tent, and cook for an additional 5 minutes; during the last 2 minutes of grilling, top each with a slice of mozzarella.
4. Remove steaks from the griddle and top each with a few tomato slices, and 2 basil leaves.
5. Drizzle with balsamic, sprinkle with sea salt and black pepper, and serve.

4 (6 ounces) filets
1 teaspoon garlic salt
1 tbsp Italian Olive oil
2 Roma tomatoes, sliced
4 ounces fresh buffalo mozzarella, cut into four slices
8 fresh basil leaves
1 tbsp Balsamic vinegar glaze for drizzling
Sea salt for seasoning
Fresh ground pepper

Nutrition: Calories: 406, Fat: 22 g, Carbs: 7 g, Protein: 45 g

88

Tender Steak with Pineapple Rice

 Prep Time 10 min   **Cook Time** 25 min   **Servings** 4

4 (4-ounce) beef fillets
1/4 cup soy sauce
1/2 teaspoon black pepper
1/2 teaspoon garlic powder
1 (8-ounce) can of pineapple chunks, in juice, drained
2 scallions, thin sliced
2 (8.8-ounce) packages of pre-cooked brown rice, like Uncle Ben's
7/8 teaspoon kosher salt
Olive oil, for brushing

1. Combine soy sauce, pepper, garlic powder, and beef in a large sealable plastic bag.
2. Seal and massage sauce into beef; let stand at room temperature for 7 minutes, turning bag occasionally.
3. Preheat the griddle to medium-high heat and brush with olive oil.
4. Add pineapple and green onions to the griddle and cook for 5 minutes or until well charred, turning to char evenly.
5. Remove pineapple mix and brush with additional olive oil.
6. Add steaks and cook for 3 minutes on each side, for rare, or until the desired temperature is reached.
7. Cook rice according to package instructions.
8. Add rice, pineapple, onions, and salt to a bowl and stir gently to combine.
9. Plate steaks with pineapple rice and serve!

Nutrition: Calories: 369, Fat: 12 g, Carbs: 37 g, Protein: 28 g

Texas-Style Brisket

Prep Time	Cook Time	Servings
20 min	6 h & 36 min	2

1 (4 1/2 lbs.) flat-cut beef brisket (about 3 inches thick)

For the rub:
1 tablespoon sea salt
1 tablespoon dark brown sugar
2 teaspoons smoked paprika
2 teaspoons chili powder
1 teaspoon garlic powder
1 teaspoon onion powder
1 teaspoon ground black pepper
1 teaspoon mesquite liquid smoke, like Colgin

1. Combine the rub ingredients in a small mixing bowl.
2. Rinse and pat brisket dry and rub with the coffee mix.
3. Preheat the griddle for two-zone cooking; heat one side to high and leave the other with low heat.
4. Sear on the high heat side for 3 - 5 minutes on each side or until nicely charred.
5. Move to low heat side, tent with foil, and cook for 6 hours or until a meat thermometer registers 195°F.
6. Remove from griddle. Let stand, covered, for 30 minutes.
7. Cut brisket across grain into thin slices and serve.

Nutrition: Calories: 591, Fat: 42 g, Carbs: 3 g, Protein: 45 g

---

Flank Steak with Garlic and Rosemary

Prep Time	Cook Time	Servings
15 min	24 min	2

2 (8 ounces) flank steaks
For the marinade:
1 tablespoon extra-virgin olive oil, plus more for brushing
2 tablespoons fresh rosemary, chopped
4 cloves garlic, minced
2 teaspoons sea salt
1/4 teaspoon black pepper

1. Add marinade ingredients to a food processor or blender and pulse until garlic and rosemary are pulverized.
2. Use a fork to pierce the steaks 10 times on each side.
3. Rub each evenly with the marinade on both sides.
4. Place in a covered dish and refrigerate for at least 1 hour or overnight.
5. Preheat the griddle to high and brush with olive oil and preheat to high.
6. Cook steaks for 5 minutes, flip, tent with foil, and cook for about 3-4 minutes more.
7. Transfer meat to rest on a cutting board, and cover with aluminum foil for about 15 minutes.
8. Slice very thin against the grain and serve immediately.

Nutrition: Calories: 260, Fat: 13 g, Carbs: 0 g, Protein: 23 g

---

Coffee Crusted Skirt Steak

Prep Time	Cook Time	Servings
10 min	25 min	1

1/4 cup coffee beans, finely ground
1/4 cup dark brown sugar, firmly packed
1 1/2 teaspoon sea salt
1/8 teaspoon ground cinnamon
Pinch cayenne pepper
2 1/2 lb. skirt steak, cut into 4 pieces
1 tablespoon olive oil

1. Heat griddle to high.
2. Combine coffee, brown sugar, salt, cinnamon, and cayenne pepper in a bowl to make a rub.
3. Remove steak from refrigerator and let come to room temperature, about 15 minutes. Rub steak with oil, and sprinkle with spice rub. Massage spice rub into meat.
4. Sear until charred and medium-rare, 2 to 4 minutes per side. Transfer to a cutting board, cover with foil and let rest for 5 minutes before thinly slicing against the grain.

Nutrition: Calories: 324, Fat: 16 g, Carbs: 4 g, Protein: 37 g

4 (6 ounces) flank steaks
Sea salt for seasoning
Flakey sea salt, for serving
Fresh ground pepper
Olive oil
2 Roma tomatoes, sliced
4 ounces fresh buffalo mozzarella, cut into four slices
8 fresh basil leaves
Balsamic vinegar glaze for drizzling

Caprese Flank Steak

 Prep Time 10 min   **Cook Time** 10 min   **Servings** 4

1. Lightly brush each filet, on all sides, with olive oil and season with salt and pepper.
2. Preheat the griddle to high. Place steaks on the griddle, reduce heat to medium, tent with foil, and cook for 5 minutes.
3. Flip, re-tent, and cook for an additional 5 minutes; during the last 2 minutes of cooking, top each with a slice of mozzarella.
4. Remove steaks from the griddle and top each with a few tomato slices, and 2 basil leaves.
5. Drizzle with balsamic glaze, and sprinkle with flakey salt and a little more black pepper.

Nutrition: Calories: 461, Fat: 23 g, Carbs: 6 g, Protein: 56 g

2 (8 ounces) skirt steaks
For the marinade:
2 tablespoons balsamic vinegar
2 teaspoons olive oil, more for brushing
2 garlic cloves, minced
Sea salt, to taste
Black pepper, to taste

Flash-Marinated Skirt Steak

 Prep Time 5 min   **Cook Time** 15 min   **Servings** 2

1. Combine marinade ingredients in a sealable plastic bag, add steaks, seal bag, turn to coat, and let stand at room temperature for 30 minutes.
2. Preheat the griddle to medium-high heat.
3. Remove steaks and discard marinade, place on griddle and cook about 3 minutes per side. Transfer steaks to cutting board and rest for 5 Minutes.
4. Cut across the grain into slices and serve with your favorite sides.

Nutrition: Calories: 256, Fat: 14 g, Carbs: 1 g, Protein: 30 g

Mexican Steak Salad

Prep Time 5 min | Cook Time 10 min | Servings 2

Steak marinade:
2 tablespoons olive oil
3 garlic cloves, minced
2 teaspoons chili powder
1 teaspoon ground cumin
1 teaspoon kosher salt
1 teaspoon freshly ground pepper
1 1/2 pounds skirt or flap steak, cut into 4-inch lengths
1/2 cup lager beer

Salad:
12 ounces romaine hearts, trimmed and chopped
1 can of black beans, drained and rinsed
1-pint cherry tomatoes halved
1 large ripe avocado, pitted, peeled, and cut into chunks
About 1/3 cup crumbled queso fresco
Chopped fresh cilantro for garnish
Kosher salt

Dressing:
1/2 cup plain whole-milk yogurt
1/3 cup chopped fresh cilantro
Zest of 1 lime
Juice of 2 limes

1. Make marinade, then marinate the steak overnight.
2. Combine salad ingredients in a large bowl; add dressing and mix well. Place salad on separate plates.
3. Preheat the griddle to high. Place marinated steak on the griddle, reduce heat to medium, tent with foil, and cook for 5 minutes.
4. Flip, re-tent, and cook for an additional 5 minutes.
5. Remove steak from the griddle and slice into 2-inch strips.
6. Place steak strips on individual salads, and sprinkle with flakey salt and a little black pepper. Garnish with cilantro.

Nutrition: Calories: 780, Fat: 65 g, Carbs: 29 g, Protein: 84 g

---

4 (8-ounce / 227-g) filet mignon steaks, 2 inches thick
Salt and pepper, for coating
1/2 cup (1 stick) butter
Herb Mayo:
1/2 cup minced mixed fresh herbs, such as parsley, basil, and mint
2 tablespoons minced fennel fronds (may substitute minced tarragon leaves)
1 teaspoon lemon zest
1 cup mayonnaise
Salt, for seasoning

Filet Mignon with Herb Mayo

Prep Time 5 min | Cook Time 20 min | Servings 4

1. Wipe the griddle with oil to prevent sticking. Build a two-zone fire. Your high-heat zone should have embers 1 to 2 inches from the cooking surface, with occasional flames licking it. To create your medium-heat zone, nudge the embers 2 to 3 inches lower than that.
2. Coat the steaks generously with salt and pepper. Heat a Plancha or cast-iron griddle over high heat. Add the butter, and when it starts to smell nutty and turn color, add the steaks and turn them in the butter to coat. Sear on all sides until a dark crust forms, 2 to 3 minutes per side. Transfer to the griddle over medium heat and let cook, turning often, until an instant-read meat thermometer, placed in the thickest part of one steak, reads 125°F (52°C). Transfer to a platter and let the steaks rest for 10 minutes before serving.
3. While the meat is cooking, make the mayo: In a small bowl, mix the herbs, fennel, and lemon zest into the mayonnaise and season with salt. Serve the steaks with the mayo on the side.

Nutrition: Calories: 434, Fat: 6 g, Carbs: 10 g, Protein: 6 g

Coriander–Ancho Rub:
2 tablespoons coriander seeds
4 ancho chiles, stemmed, seeded, and roughly torn
2 teaspoons salt
1 tablespoon honey
Gribiche:
4 hard-boiled eggs, peeled and minced
2 tablespoons minced parsley leaves
2 tablespoons minced shallots
Zest and juice of 1 lemon (about 3 table-spoons juice)
1/2 cup oil
Salt and pepper, for seasoning
2 pounds (907 g) skirt steak (ask your butcher for an "outside skirt")

Skirt Steak with Chiles

 Prep Time 25 min   **Cook Time** 30 min   **Servings** 2

1. Wipe the griddle with oil to prevent sticking. Build a two-zone fire. Your high-heat zone should have embers 1 to 2 inches from the cooking surface, with occasional flames licking it. To create your medium-heat zone, nudge the embers 2 to 3 inches lower than that.

2. To make the rub: Place the coriander and chiles in a skillet over medium heat and stir until toasted and fragrant but not burnt, 3 to 5 minutes. Cool slightly and blend to a fine powder in a blender or food processor. Mix with salt and honey. The rub will keep tightly covered in the refrigerator for up to 2 weeks.

3. To make the gribiche: Combine the eggs, parsley, shallots, lemon zest, and juice in a bowl. Slowly add the oil while whisking constantly. Season with salt and pepper. Gribiche can be covered and refrigerated for up to 8 hours but should be served on the day it's made.

4. Coat the steaks liberally with the rub. Let them rest uncovered in the refrigerator for at least 1 hour and up to 4 hours. Place the steak over high heat for about 90 seconds, then turn 45°F and cook for another 90 seconds. Flip and repeat on the other side for a total of 6 minutes. Move to medium heat and test for doneness by slicing it into one steak; you don't want it cooked beyond medium-rare. Transfer steak to a cutting board, let rest for 5 minutes, then slice against the grain and serve with the gribiche.

Nutrition:Calories: 490, Fat: 4 g, Carbs: 26 g, Protein: 26 g

Beef Steak with Salt

 Prep Time 25 min   **Cook Time** 45 min   **Servings** 7

2 porterhouse steaks, about 11/2 inches thick
Butcher's salt, for coating

1. Wipe the griddle with oil to prevent sticking. Build a high-heat fire. Your high-heat zone should have embers 1 to 2 inches from the cooking surface, with occasional flames licking it.

2. Pat the steaks dry and coat them with salt. Let sit for 20 to 30 minutes. Place the steaks over high heat. Cook for about 2 minutes, then turn the steaks 45°F and cook for another 2 minutes. Flip and repeat on the other side. Cook, flipping occasionally, until an instant-read meat thermometer, placed in the thickest part of one steak, reads 125°F (52°C) (this shouldn't take much longer than 8 to 10 minutes total). Transfer to a cutting board and let rest for 10 minutes before slicing and serving.

Nutrition: Calories: 248, Carb: 25 g, Protein: 29 g, Fat: 3 g

Carne Asada

Prep Time 5 min **Cook Time** 16 min **Servings** 1

1 lb. hanger steak or shirt steak
1/4 cup olive oil
1 lime, juiced
1 orange, juiced
1 garlic clove, finely chopped
1/2 teaspoon cumin
1/4 teaspoon salt
1/4 teaspoon ground pepper
A handful of fresh cilantro, chopped

1. Combine all of the ingredients in a large sealable plastic bag. Marinate in the refrigerator for 1 to 2 hours.
2. Preheat to medium/high heat, and cook for 3 minutes on each side or until just cooked through.
3. Transfer to cutting board to rest for 10 minutes.
4. Slice against the grain and serve.

Nutrition: Calories: 363, Fat: 18 g, Carbs: 8 g, Protein: 42 g

Rib Roast with Potato

Prep Time 15 min **Cook Time** 40 min **Servings** 6

1 (4- to 5-pound / 1.8- to 2.3-kg) standing rib roast
Salt and pepper, for seasoning
1 apple, of any variety
2 large shallots
1 large bunch of mixed herbs (with stems), such as rosemary, sage, tarragon, and parsley, tied at the base to make a "broom"

6 to 8 large russet potatoes (at least 1 per person)
1/4 cup store-bought black garlic, peeled
2 cups sour cream

1. Season the roast generously with salt and pepper and let it sit, covered, at room temperature for 2 hours before cooking. This will bring the meat to room temperature all the way through, so you don't risk having cool meat at the center after cooking.
2. Meanwhile, wipe the griddle with oil to prevent sticking. Build a medium-heat fire. Your medium-heat zone should have embers 3 to 5 inches from the cooking surface.
3. Place the roast bone side down over medium heat and put the apple and shallots directly in the embers. After about 30 minutes, start turning the roast occasionally, so that every exposed part gets deeply browned (the bone side should get the most time on the griddle since that meat takes longer to cook).
4. As the roast browns and the Fat: renders from the surface, brush the roast firmly with the herb broom, allowing some of the leaves to fall onto the roast and into the fire (let the herbs sit on the griddle when you're not using them). When the shallot and apple are very soft and almost falling apart, use tongs to rub them all over the roast as it cooks. You want to build up a shallot-apple-herb crust that will both flavor and protect the meat.
5. After about 1 hour, put the potatoes in the embers under the roast so they catch some of the drippings. No need to prick the potatoes; if any of them explode, which is unlikely, it makes a good story, and they'll absorb more of the tasty beef fat. The roast should take about 2 hours to cook through (move it to higher heat if it's not building up a deeply colored crust), but after about 90 minutes, start checking the temperature with an instant-read meat thermometer. Cook to an internal temperature of 130°F (54°C) (because of its ample Fat: marbling, rib roast is best when it's not too rare).
6. Remove the roast to a cutting board using potholder-covered hands or two large forks. Tent with aluminum foil and let it rest for 20 to 30 minutes. When the potatoes can be easily pierced with a butter knife, use tongs to remove them, wrap them with foil, and leave them on a corner of the griddle to keep warm.
7. While the roast is resting, mash the black garlic with a fork in a bowl until very smooth. Add the sour cream and whisk until smooth and fluffy. Using scissors, snip the herbs from the herb broom directly into the sauce.
8. Remove the potatoes from the foil and arrange them around the roast on the platter. To serve, carve the roast at the table and pass the sauce alongside.

Nutrition: Calories: 363, Fat: 18 g, Carbs: 8 g, Protein: 42 g

Beef Short Ribs with Carrot

Prep Time 15 min **Cook Time** 6h&10 min **Servings** 5

Rub:
3 chipotle chiles, toasted, stemmed and seeded
3 Pasilla chiles, toasted, stemmed and seeded
1 tablespoon salt
1 tablespoon fennel seeds, ground
1 tablespoon sugar
1 tablespoon honey
1 tablespoon roasted garlic
5 pounds (2.3 kg) of bone-in beef short ribs
Salt, for seasoning
2 white onions, coarsely chopped
2 carrots, coarsely chopped
3 celery stalks, coarsely chopped
Celery Root and Horseradish Slaw, for serving

Nutrition: Calories: 249, Carbs: 2 g, Fat: 19 g, Protein: 24 g

1. Prepare the griddle and bring it to between 220° and 240°F. To make the rub: Grind the chiles to a powder in a blender or spice grinder, then transfer to a bowl together with the salt, fennel, sugar, honey, and garlic (the mixture should resemble wet sand). The rub can be made ahead, covered, and refrigerated for up to 1 week.

2. Score the tops of the short ribs, season liberally with salt, and then coat with the rub. Pack any extra rub on top of the short ribs and place the ribs, meat side up, directly on a shelf in the griddle. Cook for 6 hours.

3. Wipe the griddle with oil to prevent sticking. Build a two-zone fire. Your high-heat zone should have embers 1 to 2 inches from the cooking surface, with occasional flames licking it. To create your medium-heat zone, nudge the embers 2 to 3 inches lower than that.

4. Using tongs, transfer the ribs to a Dutch oven and add the onions, carrots, celery, and enough water to cover three-quarters of the ribs. Cover tightly and place on the griddle over medium heat for 3 hours. Remove the ribs and set them aside. Strain the broth through a medium-mesh strainer, discard the vegetables, and skim the Fat: from the surface. Return the broth to the pot and bring it to a boil over high heat. Reduce by about half and then return the ribs to the pan. Continue reducing the sauce while turning the ribs occasionally until the sauce becomes a glaze for the ribs. Remove the bones from the ribs, transfer the ribs and sauce to a serving platter, and serve immediately, with the slaw on the side.

Lamb Shoulder Chops

Prep Time 5 min **Cook Time** 30 min **Servings** 4

4 (8- to 12-ounce / 227- to 340-g) lamb shoulder chops (blade or round bone) ¾ to 1 inch thick, trimmed
2 tablespoons extra-virgin olive oil
Salt and pepper, to taste

1. Turn all burners to high, cover, and heat the griddle until hot, about 15 minutes. Leave the primary burner on high and turn another burner to medium.

2. Clean and oil cooking grate. Rub chops with oil and season with salt and pepper. Place chops on the hotter side of the griddle and cook (covered if using gas) until well browned, about 2 minutes per side. Slide chops to the cooler side of the griddle and continue to cook until meat registers 120°F (49°C) to 125°F (52°C) (for medium-rare) or 130°F (54°C) to 135°F (57°C) (for medium), 2 to 4 minutes per side. Transfer chops to a large platter, tent with aluminum foil, and let rest for 5 minutes before serving.

Nutrition: Calories: 331, Fat: 13 g, Carbs: 3 g, Protein: 5 g

Rib Eye Steak with Butter

Prep Time 20 min   **Cook Time** 60 min   **Servings** 2

1 unpeeled white or red onion
Oil, for coating
1 tablespoon molasses (may substitute honey)
1 tablespoon butter
Salt, for seasoning and coating
1 (1-pound / 454-g) bone-in rib-eye steak, about 1 1/2 inches thick
Pepper, for coating

1. Wipe the griddle with oil to prevent sticking. Build a two-zone fire. Your high-heat zone should have embers 1 to 2 inches from the cooking surface, with occasional flames licking it. To create your medium-heat zone, nudge the embers 2 to 3 inches lower than that.
2. Roast the onion directly in the embers until it feels soft when prodded with tongs, about 20 minutes. Transfer to a cutting board, remove the skin and chop the flesh finely. Coat a small cast-iron pan with oil and place over medium heat. Add the onion and cook until it's a deep brown. Add the molasses and cook for another 5 minutes, then add the butter, season with salt, and keep the sauce warm on a corner of the griddle while you cook the rib eye.
3. Coat the steak generously with salt and pepper and let sit for 20 to 30 minutes. Place over high heat and sear for about 6 minutes per side, turning often, until it's deeply browned. Remove from heat when an instant-read meat thermometer, placed in the thickest part, reads 130°F (54°C). Transfer to a serving plate and let sit for 10 minutes before eating with the caramelized onions.

Nutrition: Calories: 298, Fat: 12 g, Carbs: 26 g, Protein: 18 g

Steak with Cheese

Prep Time 10 min   **Cook Time** 46 min   **Servings** 2

1 (24-ounce / 680-g) dry-aged New York strip steak
salt and pepper, for coating
1/2 cup blue cheese, such as Roquefort, Gorgonzola, Bleu D'auvergne, or Danish blue
2 tablespoons oil

1. Wipe the griddle with oil to prevent sticking. Build a two-zone fire. Your high-heat zone should have embers 1 to 2 inches from the cooking surface, with occasional flames licking it. To create your medium-heat zone, nudge the embers 2 to 3 inches lower than that.
2. Pat the steak dry and coat it with salt and pepper. Let sit for 20 to 30 minutes. Place the steak over high heat for 5 minutes, then flip and repeat. Move to medium heat and cook for another 2 to 3 minutes until an instant-read meat thermometer, placed in the thickest part of the steak, reads 125°F (52°C). Transfer to a cutting board and let rest for 10 minutes.
3. While the steak is cooling, combine the cheese and oil in a food processor and blend until smooth and fluffy, about 1 minute. Slice the steak against the grain and top with the blue cheese mixture just before serving

Nutrition: Calories: 295, Carbs: 28 g, Fat: 17 g, Protein: 3 g

New York Strip with Sauce

Prep Time 5 min **Cook Time** 20 min **Servings** 4

3 poblano chiles
2 white or red unpeeled onions, halved
Oil and salt, for coating
3 tablespoons vinegar
2 tablespoons soy sauce
1 tablespoon freshly squeezed lime juice
1 tablespoon roasted garlic
1 tablespoon honey
2 pounds (907 g) New York strip steak

Nutrition Calories: 229, Carbs: 2 g, Fat: 13 g, Protein: 24 g

1. Wipe the griddle with oil to prevent sticking. Build a high-heat fire. Your high-heat zone should have embers 1 to 2 inches from the cooking surface, with occasional flames licking it.

2. To make the sauce: Toss the poblanos and onions in oil and salt. Cook over high heat, turning occasionally until they are completely blackened, about 10 minutes for the poblanos and a little longer for the onions. Transfer with tongs to a bowl, then tightly cover with plastic wrap to allow them to steam in their heat and to cool enough to handle. Peel the skin from the chiles with your fingers, but don't worry if some burnt bits remain. Remove and discard the stems and seeds. Cut the peel and root end from the onions.

3. Place the chiles and onions in a blender together with the vinegar, soy sauce, lime juice, garlic, and honey and blend until completely smooth. The sauce can be stored in a covered container in the refrigerator for up to 2 weeks.

4. Coat the steaks generously with the sauce and let them marinate for 1 hour. Place the steaks over high heat and grill for about 5 minutes per side until an instant-read meat thermometer, placed in the thickest part of one steak, reads 125°F (52°C). Use tongs to sear the edges of the meat as well. Transfer to a cutting board and let rest for 10 minutes. Slice against the grain and serve, passing additional sauce at the table.

Lamb Chops with BBQ Sauce

Prep Time 20 min **Cook Time** 20 min **Servings** 8

10 large tomatillos, peeled and rinsed
5 jalapeño chiles
2 cups vinegar
2 cups water
¾ cup sugar
1 tablespoon salt
2 1/2 pounds (1.1 kg) lamb ribs or loin chops, each at least 1 inch thick
Salt, for seasoning

Nutrition Calories: 503, Fat: 18 g, Carbs: 54 g, Protein: 30 g

1. Wipe the griddle with oil to prevent sticking. Build a two-zone fire. Your high-heat zone should have embers 1 to 2 inches from the cooking surface, with occasional flames licking it. To create your medium-heat zone, nudge the embers 2 to 3 inches lower than that.

2. To make the sauce: Place the tomatillos and jalapeños over medium heat, turning occasionally, until slightly charred all over, about 8 minutes total. Transfer to a plate and cut the tomatillos in half, reserving the juice. Halve the jalapeños lengthwise, remove the stems, and scrape out some of the seeds and veins. Combine the tomatillos (with their juice) and jalapeños with the vinegar, water, sugar, and salt in a medium saucepan and simmer over low heat for 20 to 30 minutes, until the sauce is reduced and slightly syrupy. Cool the mixture slightly, transfer to a blender, and blend until very smooth. The sauce can be covered and refrigerated for up to 1 week.

3. Salt the chops well, then place them over high heat and sear on all sides (use tongs to crisp up the Fat: on the edges), about 2 minutes per side. Move to medium heat and cook, often turning, until just past medium-rare (about 135°F (57°C) on an instant-read meat thermometer), about 5 minutes more in total. Transfer to a serving platter and let rest for 5 minutes before serving, passing the sauce separately.

Lamb Chops with Apricot

Prep Time 5 min   **Cook Time** 15 min   **Servings** 8

2 Apricot–Chamomile Chutney
Oil, for coating
1 white or red onion, chopped
1 cup dried apricots, chopped
1 tablespoon dried chamomile, plus more for garnish
2 whole star anise
3 green or white cardamom pods, with seeds removed
1/4 cup honey, plus more for garnish
1 cup water
2 tablespoons chopped mint leaves
2 tablespoons chopped toasted unsalted almonds
Juice of 1 lemon (about 3 tablespoons)
21/2 pounds (1.1 kg) lamb loin chops, at least 1 inch thick
Salt, for seasoning

Nutrition: Calories: 407, Fat: 34 g, Carbs: 5 g, Protein: 54 g

1. Wipe the griddle with oil to prevent sticking. Build a two-zone fire. Your high-heat zone should have embers 1 to 2 inches from the cooking surface, with occasional flames licking it. To create your medium-heat zone, nudge the embers 2 to 3 inches lower than that.
2. To make the chutney: Coat a sauté pan with oil and place over medium heat. Add the onion and cook until tender, about 5 minutes. Add the apricots, chamomile, star anise, cardamom, honey, and water. Cook until almost all of the liquid has cooked off and the mixture is thick and syrupy. (The mixture can be made to this stage up to 5 days in advance and refrigerated in a covered container.) Discard the star anise. Stir in the mint, almonds, and lemon juice.
3. Score the fatty edge of each lamb chop by cutting shallow crosshatched slices into it.
4. Salt the chops well, then place them over high heat and sear on all sides (use tongs to crisp up the Fat: on the edges), about 2 minutes per side. Move to medium heat and cook, turning often, until just past medium-rare (about 135°F (57°C) on an instant-read meat thermometer), about 5 minutes more in total. Transfer to a serving platter and drizzle with honey, sprinkle with chamomile and serve with warm chutney alongside.

1 (8 ounce / 227 g) NY strip steak
Olive oil
Sea salt and fresh ground black pepper, to taste

Nutrition: Calories: 141, Fat: 11 g, Carbs: 5 g, Protein: 23 g

Strip Steak with Pepper

Prep Time 5 min   **Cook Time** 15 min   **Servings** 7

1. Remove the steak from the refrigerator and let it come to room temperature, about 30 to 45 minutes.
2. Preheat the griddle to medium-high heat and brush with olive oil.
3. Season the steak on all sides with salt and pepper.
4. Cook steak for about 4 to 5 minutes.
5. Flip and cook about 4 minutes more for medium-rare steak; between 125°F (52°C) and 130°F (54°C) on a meat thermometer.
6. Transfer the steak to a plate and let it rest for 5 minutes before serving.

Lamb Loin Rib Chops

 Prep Time 15 min **Cook Time** 40 min **Servings** 8

8 (4-ounce / 113-g) lamb rib or loin chops
11/4 to 11/2 inches thick, trimmed
2 tablespoons extra-virgin olive oil
Salt and pepper, to taste

Nutrition: Calories: 345, Fat: 8 g, Carbs: 10 g, Protein: 10 g

1. Turn all burners to high, cover, and heat the griddle until hot, about 15 minutes. Leave the primary burner on high and turn the other one(s) to medium.
2. Clean and oil cooking grate. Rub chops with oil and season with salt and pepper. Place chops on the hotter side of the griddle and cook (covered if using gas) until well browned, about 2 minutes per side. Slide chops to the cooler side of the griddle and continue to cook until meat registers 120°F (49°C) to 125°F (52°C) (for medium-rare) or 130°F (54°C) to 135°F (57°C) (for medium), 2 to 4 minutes per side. Transfer chops to a large platter, tent with aluminum foil, and let rest for 5 minutes before serving

2 (1 pound / 454 g) sirloin steaks
1 tablespoon garlic powder
4 tablespoons soy sauce
1 white onion, sliced into large rounds
3 zucchini, sliced into 1/4 inch thick flats
2 cups snap peas
4 tablespoons vegetable oil
3 tablespoons butter
Salt and black pepper, to taste

Beef Steaks with Zucchini

 Prep Time 5 min **Cook Time** 15 min **Servings** 8

1. Season the steak with salt, pepper, and garlic powder.
2. Set your griddle to high heat on one side and medium-high heat on the other side.
3. Add some vegetable oil to the medium-hot side and add the onion rings, zucchini, and snap peas. Season with a little salt and pepper.
4. Add the steaks to the hot side and cook for 3 minutes. Flip, top with butter, and add soy sauce to the steaks. Continue cooking for additional 4 minutes.
5. Remove the steak and vegetables from the griddle and slice the steak across the grain before serving.

Nutrition Calories: 503, Fat: 18 g, Carbs: 54 g, Protein: 30 g

Lamb Kofte with Sauce

 Prep Time 15 min   **Cook Time** 60 min   **Servings** 8

4 teaspoons vegetable oil
4 teaspoons minced fresh rosemary
2 teaspoons minced fresh thyme
2 garlic cloves, minced
2 (11/2- to 1¾-pound / 680- to 794-g) racks of lamb (8 ribs each), trimmed and frenched
Salt and pepper, to taste

1. Combine 1 tablespoon oil, rosemary, thyme, and garlic in a bowl; set aside. Pat lamb dry with paper towels, rub with remaining 1 teaspoon oil, and season with salt and pepper.
2. Turn all burners to high, cover, and heat the griddle until hot, about 15 minutes. Leave the primary burner on high and turn off another burner.
3. Clean and oil cooking grate. Place lamb, bone side up, on the cooler part of the griddle with meaty side of racks very close to, but not quite over, hot coals or lit burner. Cover and cook until meat is lightly browned, and Fat: has begun to render, 8 to 10 minutes.
4. Flip racks bone side down and slide to a hotter part of the griddle. Cook until well browned, 3 to 4 minutes. Brush racks with herb mixture, flip bone side up and cook until well browned, 3 to 4 minutes. Stand racks up, leaning them against each other for support, and cook until the bottom is well browned and meat registers 120°F (49°C) to 125°F (52°C) (for medium-rare) or 130°F (54°C) to 135°F (57°C) (for medium), 3 to 8 minutes.
5. Transfer lamb to carving board, tent with aluminum foil, and let rest for 15 to 20 minutes. Cut between ribs to separate chops and serve.

Nutrition: Calories: 125, Fat: 12 g, Carbs: 1 g, Protein: 5.8 g

Beef Steaks with Zucchini

2 (1-pound / 454-g) New York strip steaks, trimmed
The Rub:
1 bunch of thyme sprigs
1 bunch of rosemary sprigs
1 bunch of sage sprigs
1 1/2 teaspoons black pepper, divided
¾ teaspoon sea salt, divided
1/2 teaspoon garlic powder
2 tablespoons chopped fresh flat-leaf parsley
2 tablespoons extra-virgin olive oil

Prep Time 5 min   **Cook Time** 15 min   **Servings** 8

1. Preheat the griddle to high heat.
2. Combine rub ingredients in a small mixing bowl and rub steaks with spice mixture; let rest for 10 minutes.
3. Place steaks on the griddle and cook for 1 minute per side.
4. Turn the griddle down to medium heat.
5. Turn steaks and cook for 3 additional minutes per side; or until the thermometer registers 135°F for medium-rare.
6. Remove steaks to a platter.
7. Let rest for 5 minutes. Cut steaks across the grain into thin slices.

Nutrition: Calories: 102, Fat: 6 g, Carbs: 2 g, Protein: 9 g

Game Recipes

Rosemary Hen

 Prep Time 15 min   **Cook Time** 60 min   **Servings** 5

1. Brush hens with melted butter.
2. Mix rosemary and chicken rub.
3. Rub hen with rosemary and chicken rub mixture.
4. Preheat the griddle to high heat.
5. Spray griddle top with cooking spray.
6. Place hen on hot griddle top and cook for 60 minutes or until internal temperature reaches 165°F.
7. Serve and enjoy.

1 Cornish game hen
1 tablespoon butter, melted
1/2 tablespoon rosemary, minced
1 teaspoon chicken rub

Nutrition: Calories: 221, Fat: 17 g, Carbs: 1 g, Protein: 14 g

Flavorful Marinated Cornish Hen

 Prep Time 5 min   **Cook Time** 60 min   **Servings** 5

1 Cornish hen
1 cup cold water
16 oz apple juice
1/8 cup brown sugar
1 cinnamon stick
1 cup hot water
1/4 cup kosher salt

1. Add cinnamon, hot water, cold water, apple juice, brown sugar, and salt into the large pot and stir until sugar is dissolved.
2. Add hen in the brine and place in the refrigerator for 4 hours.
3. Preheat the griddle to high heat.
4. Spray griddle top with cooking spray.
5. Remove hens from brine, place on hot griddle top, and cook for 60 minutes or until internal temperature reaches 160°F.
6. Slice and serve.

Nutrition: Calories: 938, Fat: 9 g, Carbs: 232 g, Protein: 10 g

Montreal Seasoned Spatchcocked Hens

1. Cut the backbone of the hens and flatten the breastplate.
2. Brush the hen with oil and rub it with Montreal chicken seasoning.
3. Wrap hens in plastic wrap and place them in the refrigerator for 4 hours.
4. Preheat the griddle to high heat.
5. Spray griddle top with cooking spray.
6. Place marinated hen on hot griddle top and cook for 60 minutes or until internal temperature reaches 180°F.
7. Serve and enjoy

 Prep Time 25 min   **Cook Time** 60 min   **Servings** 6

1 Cornish hen
1 tablespoon olive oil
1 tablespoon Montreal chicken seasoning

Nutrition: Calories: 938, Fat: 9 g, Carbs: 232 g, Protein: 10 g

Orange Cornish Hen

 Prep Time 35 min   **Cook Time** 60 min   **Servings** 6

1 Cornish hen
1/4 onion, cut into chunks
1/4 orange cut into wedges
2 garlic cloves
4 fresh sage leaves
1 1/2 fresh rosemary sprigs
For glaze:
2-star anise
1 tablespoon honey
1 cup orange juice
1/4 fresh orange, sliced
1/2 orange zest
1.5 oz Grand Marnier
1/2 cinnamon stick

1. Stuff hen with orange wedges, garlic, onions, and herbs. Season with pepper and salt.
2. Preheat the griddle to high heat.
3. Spray griddle top with cooking spray.
4. Place hen on hot griddle top and cook for 60 minutes or until the internal temperature of hens reaches 165°F.
5. Meanwhile, in a saucepan heat, all glaze ingredients until reduced by half over medium-high heat.
6. Brush hen with glaze.
7. Slice and serve.

Nutrition: Calories: 351, Fat: 12 g, Carbs: 29 g, Protein: 16 g

BBQ Hen

 Prep Time 20 min   **Cook Time** 90 min   **Servings** 5

1 Cornish hen
2 tablespoons BBQ rub

Nutrition: Calories: 168, Fat: 11 g, Carbs: 0 g, Protein: 14 g

1. Preheat the griddle to high heat.
2. Spray griddle top with cooking spray.
3. Coat hens with BBQ rub and place on hot griddle top and cook for 1 1/2 hours or until the internal temperature of hens reaches 165°F.
4. Slice and serve.

Tex-Mex Turkey Burgers

 Prep Time 5 min   **Cook Time** 25 min   **Servings** 8

1/3 cup finely crushed corn tortilla chips
1 egg, beaten
1/4 cup salsa
1/3 cup shredded pepper Jack cheese
Pinch salt
Freshly ground black pepper
1pound ground turkey
1 tablespoon olive oil
1 teaspoon paprika

1. Preparing the Ingredients. In a medium bowl, combine the tortilla chips, egg, salsa, cheese, salt, and pepper, and mix well.
2. Add the turkey and mix gently but thoroughly with clean hands.
3. Form the meat mixture into patties about 1/2 inch thick.
4. Brush the patties on both sides with olive oil and sprinkle with paprika.
5. Turn the control knob to the high position. When the griddle is hot, place the burgers and cook them for 14 to 16 minutes or until the meat registers at least 165°F.

Nutrition: Calories: 354, Fat: 21 g, Carbs: 0 g, Protein: 36 g

Flavorful Cornish Game Hen

 Prep Time 25 min   **Cook Time** 60 min   **Servings** 4

1. Brush the hen with oil and rub it with poultry seasoning.
2. Preheat the griddle to high heat.
3. Spray griddle top with cooking spray.
4. Place hen on hot griddle top and cook from all sides until brown.
5. Cover hen with lid or pan and cook for 60 minutes or until the internal temperature of hen reaches 180°F.
6. Slice and serve.

1 Cornish game hen
1/2 tablespoons olive oil
1/4 tablespoons poultry seasoning

Nutrition: Calories: 366, Fat: 27 g, Carbs: 1 g, Protein: 28 g

Rosemary Butter Cornish Hens

 Prep Time 15 min   **Cook Time** 10 min   **Servings** 6

1. Stuff rosemary sprigs into the hen cavity.
2. Brush the hen with melted butter and season with poultry seasoning.
3. Preheat the griddle to high heat.
4. Spray griddle top with cooking spray.
5. Place hen on hot griddle top and cook for 60 minutes or until the internal temperature of hens reaches 165°F.
6. Slice and serve.

1 Cornish hen, rinse and pat dry with paper towels
1 tablespoon butter, melted
1 rosemary sprigs
1 teaspoon poultry seasoning

Nutrition: Calories: 127, Fat: 8 g, Carbs: 0 g, Protein: 13 g

Honey Garlic Cornish Hen

Prep Time 25 min

Cook Time 60 min

Servings 7

1 Cornish hen
2 garlic cloves, minced
1/8 cup honey
1/4 cup soy sauce
3/4 cup warm water
1 tablespoon cornstarch
1/4 cup brown sugar

1. Mix soy sauce, warm water, brown sugar, garlic, cornstarch, and honey.
2. Place Cornish hen in baking dish and season with pepper and salt.
3. Pour marinade over the hen and place in the refrigerator for 10 hours.
4. Preheat the griddle to high heat.
5. Spray griddle top with cooking spray.
6. Place marinated hen on hot griddle top and cook for 60 minutes or until internal temperature reaches 165°F.
7. Serve and enjoy.

Nutrition: Calories: 338, Fat: 11 g, Carbs: 42 g, Protein: 16 g

---

Asian Cornish Hen

Prep Time 15 min

Cook Time 60 min

Servings 6

1 Cornish hen
1 1/2 teaspoons Chinese five-spice powder
1 1/2 teaspoons rice wine
1/2 teaspoon pepper
2 cups of water
3 tablespoons soy sauce
2 tablespoons sugar
Salt

1. In a large bowl, mix water, soy sauce, sugar, rice wine, five-spice, pepper, and salt.
2. Place Cornish hen in the bowl and place in the refrigerator overnight.
3. Preheat the griddle to high heat.
4. Spray griddle top with cooking spray.
5. Remove Cornish hen from marinade, place on hot griddle top, and cook for 60 minutes or until internal temperature reaches 185°F.
6. Slice and serve.

Nutrition: Calories: 233, Fat: 11 g, Carbs: 15 g, Protein: 15 g

---

Sage Thyme Cornish Hen

Prep Time 5 min

Cook Time 60 min

Servings 6

1 Cornish hen
1/2 tablespoon paprika
1/4 teaspoon pepper
1/4 teaspoon sage
1/2 teaspoon thyme
1/2 tablespoon onion powder

1. In a small bowl, mix paprika, onion powder, thyme, sage, and pepper.
2. Rub hen with paprika mixture.
3. Preheat the griddle to high heat.
4. Spray griddle top with cooking spray.
5. Place hen on hot griddle top and cook for 60 minutes or until internal temperature reaches 185°F.
6. Serve and enjoy.

Nutrition: Calories: 180, Fat: 12 g, Carbs: 2 g, Protein: 14 g

Seafood Recipes

Honey-Lime Tilapia and Corn Foil Pack

 Prep Time 5 min   **Cook Time** 15 min   **Servings** 4

1. Preheat the griddle to high.
2. Cut 4 squares of foil about 12" long.
3. Top each piece of foil with a piece of tilapia.
4. Brush tilapia with honey and top with lime, corn, and cilantro.
5. Drizzle with olive oil and season with sea salt and pepper.
6. Cook until tilapia is cooked through and corn tender, about 15 minutes.

4 fillets tilapia
2 tablespoons honey
4 limes, thinly sliced
2 ears of corn, shucked
2 tablespoons fresh cilantro leaves
1/4 cup olive oil
Kosher salt
Freshly ground black pepper

Nutrition: Calories: 319, Fat: 14 g, Carbs: 30 g, Protein: 24 g

Salmon Fillets with Basil Butter and Broccolini

 Prep Time 5 min   **Cook Time** 20 min   **Servings** 2

2 (6 ounces) salmon fillets, skin removed
2 tablespoons of butter, unsalted
2 basil leaves, minced
1 garlic clove, minced
6 ounces broccolini
2 teaspoons olive oil
Sea salt, to taste

1. Blend butter, basil, and garlic together until well-incorporated. Form into a ball and place in refrigerator until ready to serve.
2. Preheat the griddle to medium-high heat.
3. Season both sides of the salmon fillet with salt and set them aside.
4. Add broccolini, a pinch of salt, and olive oil to a bowl, toss to coat and set aside.
5. Brush griddle with olive oil, and cook salmon, skin side down, for 12 minutes. Turn the salmon and cook for an additional 4 minutes. Remove from the griddle and allow to rest while the broccolini cooks.
6. Add the broccolini to the griddle, turning occasionally, until slightly charred, about 6 minutes.
7. Top each salmon fillet with a slice of basil butter and serve with a side of broccolini.

Nutrition: Calories: 398, Fat: 26 g, Carbs: 6 g, Protein: 35 g

Spiced Snapper with Mango and Red Onion Salad

 Prep Time 5 min **Cook Time** 25 min **Servings** 3

2 red snappers, cleaned
Sea salt
1/3 cup tandoori spice
1 tablespoon of olive oil
Extra-virgin olive oil for drizzling
Lime wedges, for serving

For the salsa:
1 ripe but firm mango, peeled and chopped
1 small red onion, thinly sliced
1 bunch of cilantro, coarsely chopped
3 tablespoons fresh lime juice

Nutrition: Calories: 211, Fat: 5 g, Carbs: 18 g, Protein: 23 g

1. Toss mango, onion, cilantro, lime juice, and a big pinch of salt in a medium mixing bowl; drizzle with a bit of olive oil and toss again to coat.
2. Place snapper on a cutting board and pat dry with paper towels. Cut slashes crosswise on a diagonal along the body every 2" on both sides, with a sharp knife, cutting all the way down to the bones.
3. Season fish generously inside and out with salt. Coat fish with tandoori spice.
4. Preheat the griddle to medium-high heat and brush with oil.
5. Cook the fish for 10 minutes, undisturbed, until the skin is puffed and charred.
6. Flip and cook fish until the other side is lightly charred and the skin is puffed for about 8 to 12 minutes.
7. Transfer to a platter.
8. Top with mango salad and serve with lime wedges.

Halibut Fillets with Spinach and Olives

 Prep Time 5 min **Cook Time** 11 min **Servings** 4

4 (6 ounces) halibut fillets
1/3 cup olive oil
4 cups of baby spinach
1/4 cup lemon juice
2 ounces pitted black olives, halved
2 tablespoons flat-leaf parsley, chopped
2 teaspoons fresh dill, chopped
Lemon wedges, to serve

1. Preheat the griddle to medium heat.
2. Toss spinach with lemon juice in a mixing bowl and set aside.
3. Brush fish with olive oil and cook for 3-4 minutes per side, or until cooked through.
4. Remove from heat, cover with foil and let rest for 5 minutes.
5. Add remaining oil and cook spinach for 2 minutes, or until just wilted. Remove from heat.
6. Toss with olives and herbs, then transfer to serving plates with fish, and serve with lemon wedges.

Nutrition: Calories: 773, Fat: 36 g, Carbs: 2 g, Protein: 109 g

---

Salmon Lime Burgers

 Prep Time 15 min **Cook Time** 10 min **Servings** 2

2 hamburger buns, sliced in half
1 tablespoon cilantro, fresh minced
1/8 teaspoon fresh ground pepper
1/2 lb. Salmon fillets, skinless, cubed
1/2 tablespoon grated lime zest
1/4 teaspoon sea salt, fine ground
1-1/2 garlic cloves, minced
1/2 tablespoon Dijon mustard
1-1/2 tablespoons shallots, finely chopped
1/2 tablespoon honey
1/2 tablespoon soy sauce

1. Mix all of your ingredients in a mixing bowl, except the hamburger buns.
2. Make 2 burger patties that are 1/2-inch thick with this mixture.
3. Preheat your griddle in a medium-temperature setting.
4. Once your griddle is preheated, place the 2 patties on the griddle.
5. Cook your patties for 5 minutes per side. Serve on warm buns and enjoy!

Nutrition: Calories: 220, Fat: 15 g, Protein: 16 g, Carbs: 6 g

Griddled Oysters with Spiced Tequila Butter

 Prep Time 5 min **Cook Time** 3 min **Servings** 6

1. Combine butter ingredients in a small mixing bowl until well incorporated and set aside.
2. Preheat the griddle to high.
3. Cook the oysters for about 1 to 2 minutes.
4. Sprinkle the oysters with salt flakes.
5. Warm the butter in a microwave for 60 seconds, and spoon the warm Tequila butter over the oysters and serve.

3 dozen medium oysters, scrubbed and shucked
Flakey sea salt, for serving

For the butter:
1/4 teaspoon crushed red pepper
7 tablespoons unsalted butter
1/4 teaspoon chili oil
1 teaspoon dried oregano
2 tablespoons freshly squeezed lemon juice
2 tablespoons Tequila Blanco, like Espolon

Nutrition: Calories: 184, Fat: 15 g, Carbs: 3 g, Protein: 4 g

Gremolata Swordfish Skewers

 Prep Time 5 min **Cook Time** 20 min **Servings** 4

1. Preheat the griddle to medium-high.
2. Combine lemon zest, parsley, garlic, 1/4 teaspoon of the salt, and pepper in a small bowl with a fork to make gremolata and set aside.
3. Mix swordfish pieces with reserved lemon juice, olive oil, red pepper flakes, and remaining salt.
4. Thread swordfish and lemon slices, alternating each, onto the metal skewers.
5. Griddle the skewers for 8 to 10 minutes, flipping halfway through, or until the fish is cooked through.
6. Place skewers on a serving platter and sprinkles with gremolata.
7. Drizzle with olive oil and serve.

1-1/2 lb. skinless swordfish fillet
2 teaspoons lemon zest
3 tablespoons lemon juice
1/2 cup finely chopped parsley
2 teaspoons garlic, minced
3/4 teaspoon sea salt
1/4 teaspoon black pepper
2 tablespoons extra-virgin olive oil, plus extra for serving
1/2 teaspoon red pepper flakes
3 lemons, cut into slices

Nutrition: Calories: 333, Fat: 16 g, Carbs: 2 g, Protein: 43 g

Lump Crab Cakes

Prep Time 5 min **Cook Time** 10 min **Servings** 3

1 lb. lump crab meat
1/2 cup panko breadcrumbs
1/3 cup mayonnaise
1 egg, beaten
2 tablespoons Dijon mustard
2 teaspoons Worcestershire sauce
1/2 teaspoon paprika
1/2 teaspoon salt
1/4 teaspoon black pepper
3 tablespoons vegetable oil

1. Preheat the griddle to medium heat.
2. In a large bowl, combine the crab, breadcrumbs, mayo, egg, mustard Worcestershire sauce, paprika, salt, and pepper. Mix well to combine.
3. Form the crab mixture into 4 large balls and flatten them slightly.
4. Add the oil to the griddle and cook the crab cakes for approximately 5 minutes per side or until browned and crispy. Serve immediately.

Nutrition: Calories: 282, Fat: 27 g, Carbs: 9.g, Protein: 18 g

Spicy Griddled Jumbo Shrimp

Prep Time 5 min **Cook Time** 10 min **Servings** 3

1-1/2 pounds uncooked jumbo shrimp, peeled and deveined

For the marinade:
2 tablespoons fresh parsley
1 bay leaf, dried
1 teaspoon chili powder
1 teaspoon garlic powder
1/4 teaspoon cayenne pepper
1/4 cup olive oil
1/4 teaspoon salt
1/8 teaspoon pepper

1. Add marinade ingredients to a food processor and process until smooth.
2. Transfer marinade to a large mixing bowl.
3. Fold in shrimp and toss to coat; refrigerate, covered, for 30 minutes.
4. Thread shrimp onto metal skewers.
5. Preheat the griddle to medium heat.
6. Cook 5-6 minutes, flipping once, until shrimp turn opaque pink.
7. Serve immediately.

Nutrition: Calories: 131, Fat: 8 g, Carbs: 1 g, Protein: 13 g

Pop-Open Clams with Horseradish-Tabasco Sauce

Prep Time 10 min **Cook Time** 3 min **Servings** 4

2 dozen littleneck clams, scrubbed
4 tablespoons unsalted butter, softened
2 tablespoons horseradish, drained
1 tablespoon hot sauce, like Tabasco
1/4 teaspoon lemon zest, finely grated
1 tablespoon fresh lemon juice
1/4 teaspoon smoked paprika
Sea salt

1. Preheat the griddle to high.
2. Blend the butter with horseradish, hot sauce, lemon zest, lemon juice, paprika, and a pinch of salt.
3. Arrange the clams over high heat and griddle them until they pop open (about 60 seconds).
4. Carefully turn the clams over using tongs, so the meat side is down.
5. Cook for about 60 seconds longer until the clam juices start to simmer.
6. Transfer the clams to a serving bowl.
7. Top each with about 1/2 teaspoon of the sauce and serve.

Nutrition: Calories: 191, Fat: 12 g, Carbs: 4 g, Protein: 14 g

Mexican Shrimp Tacos

Prep Time		Cook Time		Servings
15 min		12 min		5

2 lbs. medium shrimp, peeled and deveined
8 flour tortillas, warmed
1 bag cabbage slaw
1 cup salsa
1 cup Mexican crema
For marinade:
2 tablespoons olive oil
1 tablespoon chili powder
1 tablespoon cumin
1 tablespoon garlic powder
1 tablespoon fresh lime juice
1/4 teaspoon sea salt
1/8 teaspoon fresh ground pepper

1. Preheat a griddle to medium-high.
2. Combine oil marinade in a large sealable plastic bag. Add shrimp and toss coat; let marinate in the refrigerator for 30 minutes.
3. Cook shrimp for 3 minutes on each side until cooked through.
4. Transfer to a plate.
5. Lay two tortillas on each plate. Evenly divide the shrimp, cabbage slaw, and salsa in the middle of each tortilla.
6. Drizzle with Mexican crema and serve.

Nutrition: Calories: 400, Fat: 14 g, Carbs: 30 g, Protein: 24 g

---

Scallops with Lemony Salsa Verde

Prep Time		Cook Time		Servings
15 min		2 min		3

1 tablespoon olive oil
12 large sea scallops, side muscle removed
Sea salt, for seasoning
For the Lemony Salsa Verde:
1/2 lemon, with peel, seeded, and chopped
5 tomatillos, peeled and pulsed in a blender
1 small shallot, finely chopped
1 garlic clove, finely chopped
1/4 cup olive oil
3/4 cup finely chopped fresh parsley
1/2 cup finely chopped fresh cilantro
1/4 cup chopped fresh chives
1/4 teaspoon sea salt
1/4 teaspoon black pepper

1. Toss Lemony Salsa ingredients in a small mixing bowl and set aside.
2. Preheat the griddle to medium-high and brush with olive oil.
3. Toss scallops with 1 tablespoon olive oil on a baking sheet and season with salt.
4. Add scallops to the griddle, turning once after 45 seconds to 1 minute. Cook an additional 1 minute before removing them from the griddle.
5. Serve scallops topped with Lemony Salsa Verde.

Nutrition: Calories: 267, Fat: 9 g, Carbs: 13 g, Protein: 32 g

---

Spicy Griddled Squid

Prep Time		Cook Time		Servings
15 min		5 min		6

1-1/2 lbs. Squid, prepared
Olive oil
For the marinade:
2 cloves garlic cloves, minced
1/2 teaspoon ginger, minced
3 tablespoons gochujang
3 tablespoons corn syrup
1 teaspoon yellow mustard
1 teaspoon soy sauce
2 teaspoons sesame oil
1 teaspoon sesame seeds
2 green onions, chopped

1. Preheat the griddle to medium-high heat and brush with olive oil.
2. Add the squid and tentacles to the griddle and cook for 1 minute until the bottom looks firm and opaque.
3. Turn them over and cook for another minute; straighten out the body with tongs if it curls.
4. Baste with sauce on top of the squid and cook for 2 additional minutes.
5. Flip and baste the other side, and cook for 1 minute until the sauce evaporates and the squid turns red and shiny.

Nutrition: Calories: 292, Fat: 8 g, Carbs: 25 g, Protein: 27 g

Bacon Wrapped Scallops

 Prep Time 5 min **Cook Time** 2 min **Servings** 3

12 large sea scallops, side muscle removed
8 slices of bacon
1 tablespoon vegetable oil
12 toothpicks

1. Heat your griddle to medium heat and cook the bacon until the Fat: has rendered, but the bacon is still flexible. Remove bacon from the griddle and place on paper towels.
2. Raise griddle heat to medium-high.
3. Wrap each scallop with a half slice of bacon and skewer with a toothpick to keep the bacon in place.
4. Place the scallops on the griddle and cook for 90 seconds per side. They should be lightly browned on both sides.
5. Remove from the griddle and serve immediately.

Nutrition: Calories: 315, Fat: 20 g, Carbs: 2 g, Protein: 29 g

Griddled Popcorn Shrimp

 Prep Time 5 min **Cook Time** 10 min **Servings** 7

Spice rub:
2 teaspoons garlic powder
2 teaspoons sweet paprika
1 teaspoon onion powder
1 teaspoon dried oregano
1 teaspoon cayenne pepper
1 teaspoon salt
1 teaspoon freshly ground black pepper
1 teaspoon sugar
In a large resealable plastic bag, combine the spices and shake to blend them. (The spice mix can be made ahead and kept nearly indefinitely.)
Shrimp:
11/2 pounds shelled and deveined small shrimp
1 lemon, cut into wedges

1. Preparing the ingredients
2. Add the shrimp to the plastic bag with the spice rub and shake to coat.
3. Turn the control knob to the high position. Oil the griddle and allow it to heat until the oil is shimmering but not smoking. Cook the shrimp for about 1 minute per side until they are opaque and firm to the touch.
4. Serve the shrimp immediately in a bowl garnished with lemon wedges (and with plenty of napkins).

Nutrition:Calories: 193, Fat: 52 g, Carbs: 0 g, Protein: 35 g

1/2 lb. shrimp, peeled and deveined
1 tablespoon garlic, minced
1/3 cup olives
1 cup mushrooms, sliced
2 tablespoons olive oil
1 cup tomatoes, diced
1 small onion, chopped
Pepper
Salt

Nutrition: Calories: 325, Fat: 19 g, Carbs: 12 g, Protein: 28 g

Shrimp Veggie Stir Fry

 Prep Time 15 min   **Cook Time** 5 min **Servings** 4

1. Preheat the griddle to high heat. Add oil.
2. Add onion, mushrooms, and garlic and sauté until onion soften.
3. Add shrimp and tomatoes and stir until the shrimp is cooked through.
4. Add olives and stir well.
5. Remove pan from heat and set aside for 5 minutes. Season with pepper and salt.
6. Serve and enjoy.

Parmesan Shrimp

1 lb. shrimp, peeled and deveined
2 tablespoons parmesan cheese, grated
1 tablespoon fresh lemon juice
1 tablespoon pine nuts, toasted
1 garlic clove
1/2 cup basil
1 tablespoon olive oil
Pepper
Salt

Prep Time 5 min   **Cook Time** 6 min   **Servings** 6

1. Add basil, lemon juice, cheese, pine nuts, garlic, pepper, and salt in a blender and blend until smooth.
2. Add shrimp and basil paste to a bowl and mix well.
3. Place the shrimp bowl in the fridge for 20 minutes.
4. Preheat the griddle to high heat.
5. Spray griddle top with cooking spray. Thread marinated shrimp onto skewers and place skewers on the hot griddle top.
6. Cook shrimp for 3 minutes on each side or until cooked.
7. Serve and enjoy.

Nutrition: Calories: 129, Carbs: 2 g, Fat: 7 g, Protein: 10 g

Tasty Shrimp Skewers

Prep Time 5 min   **Cook Time** 10 min   **Servings** 3

1. Add all ingredients into the mixing bowl, mix well, and place in the refrigerator for 1 hour.
2. Remove marinated shrimp from the refrigerator and thread them onto the skewers.
3. Preheat the griddle to high heat.
4. Place skewers onto the griddle top and cook for 5-7 minutes.
5. Serve and enjoy.

1 1/2 lbs. shrimp, peeled and deveined
1 tablespoon dried oregano
2 teaspoons garlic paste
2 lemon juice
1/4 cup olive oil
1 teaspoon paprika
Pepper
Salt

Nutrition: Calories: 212, Fat: 10 g, Carbs: 2 g, Protein: 26 g

Lobster Tails with Lime Basil Butter

4 lobster tails (cut in half lengthwise)
3 tablespoons olive oil
Lime wedges (to serve)
Sea salt, to taste
For the lime basil butter:
1 stick unsalted butter, softened
1/2 bunch basil, roughly chopped
1 lime, zested and juiced
2 cloves garlic, minced
1/4 teaspoon red pepper flakes

Nutrition: Calories: 430, Fat: 34 g, Carbs: 2 g, Protein: 28 g

Prep Time 5 min   **Cook Time** 9 min   **Servings** 4

1. Add the butter ingredients to a mixing bowl and combine; set aside until ready to use.
2. Preheat the griddle to medium-high heat.
3. Drizzle the lobster tail halves with olive oil and season with salt and pepper.
4. Place the lobster tails, flesh-side down, on the griddle.
5. Allow to cook until opaque, about 3 minutes, flip and cook another 3 minutes.
6. Add a dollop of the lime basil butter during the last minute of cooking.
7. Serve immediately.

Halibut

 Prep Time 15 min **Cook Time** 8 min **Servings** 3

1. Brush the halibut fillets with olive oil and sprinkle with salt and pepper.
2. Preheat the griddle to high.
3. Spray the griddle with spray oil and immediately place the halibut on the heat.
4. Cook for 2 minutes per side.
5. Turn the griddle down to medium, and cook for 2 minutes per side.
6. Sprinkle the halibut with the parmesan, and cook an additional minute before removing it from the heat.
7. Sprinkle the fillets with parsley and lemon juice, and let them relax for 5 minutes before serving.

3 Halibut fillets, cut about 1 inch thick
1 tbsp Olive oil
Sea salt and pepper
½ cup freshly grated parmesan cheese
1 tbsp freshly chopped parsley
2 tbsp fresh lemon juice

Nutrition: Calories: 223, Carbs: 10 g, Fat: 5 g, Protein: 42 g

Coconut Pineapple Shrimp Skewers

 Prep Time 20 min **Cook Time** 12 min **Servings** 6

1-1/2 pounds uncooked jumbo shrimp, peeled and deveined
1/2 cup light coconut milk
1 tablespoon cilantro, chopped
4 teaspoons Tabasco Original Red Sauce
2 teaspoons soy sauce
1/4 cup freshly squeezed orange juice
1/4 cup freshly squeezed lime juice (from about 2 large limes)
3/4 pound pineapple, cut into 1-inch chunks
Olive oil, for griddling

1. Combine the coconut milk, cilantro, Tabasco sauce, soy sauce, orange juice, and lime juice. Add the shrimp and toss to coat.
2. Cover and place in the refrigerator to marinate for 1 hour.
3. Thread shrimp and pineapple onto metal skewers, alternating each.
4. Preheat the griddle to medium heat.
5. Cook 5-6 minutes, flipping once, until shrimp turn opaque pink.
6. Serve immediately.

Nutrition: Calories: 150, Fat: 10 g, Carbs: 15 g, Protein: 2 g

6 oz can salmon, drained, remove bones, and pat dry
2 tablespoons mayonnaise
1/2 cup almond flour
1/4 teaspoons thyme
1 egg, lightly beaten
2 tablespoons olive oil
Pepper
Salt

Nutrition: Calories: 150, Fat: 10 g, Carbs: 15 g, Protein: 2 g

Healthy Salmon Patties

 Prep Time 15 min **Cook Time** 10 min **Servings** 1

1. Add salmon, thyme, egg, mayonnaise, almond flour, pepper, and salt into the mixing bowl and mix until well combined.
2. Preheat the griddle to high heat.
3. Add oil to the griddle top.
4. Make small patties from the salmon mixture and place them onto the hot griddle top, and cook for 5-6 minutes. Turn patties and cook for 3-4 minutes more.
5. Serve and enjoy.

Greek Salmon Fillets

	Prep Time	Cook Time	Servings
	5 min	6 min	2

1. Preheat the griddle to high heat.
2. In a small bowl, mix lemon juice, basil, butter, and salt.
3. Brush salmon fillets with lemon mixture and place them on the hot griddle top.
4. Cook salmon for 2-3 minutes. Flip salmon and cook for 2-3 minutes more.
5. Serve and enjoy.

2 salmon fillets
1 tablespoon fresh basil, minced
1 tablespoon butter, melted
1 tablespoon fresh lemon juice
1/8 teaspoon salt

Nutrition: Calories: 290, Fat: 17 g, Carbs: 1 g, Protein: 34 g

Crab-stuffed Trout

	Prep Time	Cook Time	Servings
	20 min	15 min	2

12 ounces crabmeat, picked over for shells and cartilage
1 cup chopped seeded fresh tomato, drained if necessary
Grated zest of 1 lemon
1 tablespoon of good-quality olive oil, plus more for brushing the fish
2 scallions, trimmed and chopped
Salt and pepper
4 8- to 10-ounce rainbow trout, cleaned and butterflied
Lemon wedges for serving

Nutrition: Calories: 150, Fat: 10 g, Carbs: 15 g, Protein: 2 g

1. Preparing the Ingredients
2. Put the crab, tomato, and lemon zest in a medium bowl. Put the oil and scallions in a small skillet over medium heat; cook, stirring occasionally until softened, 2 to 3 Minutes. Add to the crab, sprinkle with salt and pepper, toss gently, and taste and adjust the seasoning.
3. Pat the trout dry with paper towels. Brush them with oil and sprinkle with salt and pepper on both sides. Divide the crab mixture between the trout, filling their cavities. Pull the two sides closed, pushing the filling in, if needed, to keep it from spilling out.
4. Bring the griddle to high heat, Oil the griddle, and allow it to heat. Put the trout with the open side of the fish facing you, and cook until the skin browns and the fish release easily, 8 to 10 Minutes. Carefully turn the fish, using a second spatula to lower them back down to the grates. Close the lid and cook until the stuffing is heated through and a skewer or thin knife inserted at the thickest point of a fish easily pierces it all the way through, 4 to 5 Minutes. Transfer the trout to a platter and serve with lemon wedges.

Shrimp on the Barbie

	Prep Time	Cook Time	Servings
	20 min	4 min	6

3 lbs. large raw shrimp, peeled and deveined
1/2 lb. butter, melted
3 cloves garlic, minced
Zest and juice of 1 lemon
2 teaspoons sea salt
2 teaspoons black pepper
1/4 cup grated parmesan cheese

Nutrition: Calories: 325, Fat: 20 g, Carbs: 8 g, Protein: 14 g

1. Place the shrimp on skewers.
2. Mix the remaining ingredients and set them in a bowl.
3. Heat the griddle to high and cook the shrimp, brushing with the butter mixture, for 2 minutes per side until they are cooked through. They will be solid in color with white and pink tones rather than blue and gray.
4. Serve with griddled summer vegetables, griddled yellow potatoes, or griddled corn (Elote).

Lemon Garlic Shrimp

 Prep Time 15 min **Cook Time** 8 min **Servings** 5

1. Preheat the griddle to high heat.
2. Melt butter on the griddle top.
3. Add garlic and sauté for 60 seconds.
4. Add shrimp and season with pepper and salt and cook for 4-5 minutes or until it turns pink.
5. Add lemon juice and parsley and stir well and cook for 2 minutes.
6. Serve and enjoy.

1 1/2 lbs. shrimp, peeled and deveined
1 tablespoon garlic, minced
1/4 cup butter
1/4 cup fresh parsley, chopped
1/4 cup fresh lemon juice
Pepper
Salt

Nutrition: Calories: 312, Fat: 14 g, Carbs: 4 g, Protein: 39 g

Spiced Crab Legs

 Prep Time 5 min **Cook Time** 5 min **Servings** 4

4 lbs. king crab legs, cooked
2 tablespoons chili oil

1. Preheat the griddle to high.
2. Brush both sides of crab legs with chili oil and place them on the griddle. Tent with foil.
3. Cook for 4 to 5 minutes, turning once.
4. Transfer to plates and serve with drawn butter.

Nutrition: Calories: 518, Fat: 14 g, Carbs: 0 g, Protein: 87 g

Lemon Garlic Scallops

 Prep Time 10 min **Cook Time** 5 min **Servings** 3

1 lb. frozen bay scallops, thawed, rinsed and pat dry
1 teaspoon garlic, minced
2 tablespoons olive oil
1 teaspoon parsley, chopped
1 teaspoon lemon juice
Pepper
Salt

1. Preheat the griddle to high heat.
2. Add oil to the griddle top.
3. Add garlic and sauté for 30 seconds.
4. Add scallops, lemon juice, pepper, and salt, and sauté until scallops turn opaque.
5. Garnish with parsley and serve

Nutrition: Calories: 123, Fat: 14 g, Carbs: 1 g, Protein: 25 g

Dessert and Snack Recipes

Bacon Chocolate Chip Cookies

8 slices of cooked and crumbled bacon
2 1/2 teaspoon apple cider vinegar
1 teaspoon vanilla
2 cup semisweet chocolate chips
2 room temp eggs
1 1/2 teaspoon baking soda
1 cup granulated sugar
1/2 teaspoon salt
2 ¾ cup all-purpose flour
1 cup light brown sugar
1 1/2 stick softened butter

Prep Time 5 min   **Cook Time** 13 min   **Servings** 6

1. Mix salt, baking soda, and flour.
2. Cream the sugar and the butter together. Lower the speed. Add in the eggs, vinegar, and vanilla.
3. Put it on low fire, and slowly add in the flour mixture, bacon pieces, and chocolate chips.
4. Preheat your griddle, with your lid closed, until it reaches 375°F.
5. Put parchment paper on a baking sheet you are using and drop a teaspoonful of cookie batter on the baking sheet. Let them cook on the griddle, covered, for approximately 12 minutes or until they are browned

Nutrition: Calories: 221, Fat: 17 g, Carbs: 1 g, Protein: 14 g

Flavorful Marinated Cornish Hen

Prep Time 5 min   **Cook Time** 60 min   **Servings** 5

1 Cornish hen
1 cup cold water
16 oz apple juice
1/8 cup brown sugar
1 cinnamon stick
1 cup hot water
1/4 cup kosher salt

Nutrition: Calories: 938, Fat: 9 g, Carbs: 232 g, Protein: 10 g

1. Add cinnamon, hot water, cold water, apple juice, brown sugar, and salt into the large pot and stir until sugar is dissolved.
2. Add hen in the brine and place in the refrigerator for 4 hours.
3. Preheat the griddle to high heat.
4. Spray griddle top with cooking spray.
5. Remove hens from brine, place on hot griddle top, and cook for 60 minutes or until internal temperature reaches 160°F.
6. Slice and serve.

Cheesy Jalapeño Griddle Dip

 Prep Time 15 min **Cook Time** 25 min **Servings** 3

8 ounces cream cheese
16 ounces shredded cheese
1/3 cup mayonnaise
4 ounces diced green chilies
3 fresh jalapeños
2 teaspoons Killer Hogs AP Rub
2 teaspoons Mexican Style Seasoning

For the topping:
1/4 cup Mexican Blend Shredded Cheese
Sliced jalapeños
Mexican Style Seasoning
3 tablespoons Killer Hogs AP Rub
2 tablespoons Chili Powder
2 tablespoons Paprika
2 teaspoons Cumin
1/2 teaspoon Granulated Onion
1/4 teaspoon Cayenne Pepper
1/4 teaspoon Chipotle Chili Pepper ground
1/4 teaspoon Oregano

1. Preheat the griddle or flame broil for roundabout cooking at 350°F
2. Join fixings in a big bowl and spot in a cast to press griddle
3. Top with Mexican Blend destroyed Cheddar and cuts of jalapeno's
4. Spot iron griddle on flame broil mesh and cook until Cheddar is hot and bubbly and the top has seared
5. Marginally about 25 mins.
6. Serve warm with enormous corn chips (scoops), tortilla chips, or your preferred vegetables for plunging.

Nutrition: Calories: 150, Carbs: 22 g, Fat: 6 g, Protein: 3 g

White Chocolate Bread Pudding

 Prep Time 25 min **Cook Time** 31 min **Servings** 7

1 loaf of French bread
4 cups heavy cream
3 large eggs
2 cups white sugar
1 package of white chocolate morsels
1/4 cup melted butter
2 teaspoons vanilla
1 teaspoon ground nutmeg
1 teaspoon salt
Bourbon white chocolate sauce:
1 package of white chocolate morsels
1 cup heavy cream
2 tablespoons melted butter
2 tablespoons bourbon
1/2 teaspoon salt

1. Preheat the griddle to 350°F.
2. Tear French bread into little portions and spot it in a large bowl. Pour four cups of Heavy Cream over the bread and douse for 30mins.
3. Join eggs, sugar, softened spread, and vanilla in a medium to estimate bowl. Include a package of white chocolate pieces and a delicate blend. Season with Nutmeg and Salt.
4. Pour egg combo over the splashed French bread and blend to sign up for.
5. Pour the combination into a properly buttered 9x13 to an inch meal dish and spot it on the griddle.
6. Cook for 60 seconds or until the bread pudding has set and the top is darker.
7. For the sauce: Melt margarine in a saucepot over medium warm temperature. Add whiskey and hold on cooking for 3 to 4 mins until liquor vanishes and margarine begins to darkish-colored.
8. Include vast cream and heat till a mild stew. Take from the warmth and consist of white chocolate pieces a bit at a time, continuously blending until it has softened. Season with a hint of salt and serve over bread pudding.

Nutrition: Calories: 125, Fat: 12 g, Carbs: 1 g, Protein: 5.8 g

4 bananas, peeled and sliced into medallions
Cinnamon powder, as needed
Cayenne pepper, as needed
4 large scoops of vanilla ice cream
1/2 cup creamy peanut butter
Caramel sauce, as needed
Peanuts, chopped, as needed
Salted Caramel Peanut Butter Sundae
Pink sea salt, as needed

Banana Peanut Butter Sundae

 Prep Time 5 min   **Cook Time** 25 min   **Servings** 4

1. Sprinkle the bananas with cinnamon and cayenne pepper before cooking for a little kick!
2. Cook the bananas on high heat. Scoop ice cream into a serving bowl. Top with bananas, then peanut butter, caramel sauce, and chopped peanuts.
3. Sprinkle lightly with pink sea salt before serving—1/2 cup caramel sauce 1/4 cup peanuts, and chopped pink sea salt, to sprinkle.

Nutrition: Calories: 170, Carbs: 28 g, Fat: 5 g, Protein: 4 g

Spicy Sausage and Cheese Balls

 Prep Time 5 min   **Cook Time** 15 min   **Servings** 8

1 lb. hot breakfast sausage
2 cups Bisquick baking mix
8 ounces cream cheese
8 ounces of extra-sharp Cheddar cheese
1/4 cup Fresno peppers
1 tablespoon dried parsley
1 teaspoon killer hogs ap rub
1/2 teaspoon onion powder

1. Get ready the griddle for cooking at 400°F.
2. Blend Sausage, Baking Mix, destroyed Cheddar, cream Cheddar, and remaining fixings in a huge bowl until all-around fused.
3. Utilize a little scoop to parcel blend into chomp to estimate balls and roll tenderly fit as a fiddle.
4. Spot wiener and Cheddar balls on a cast-iron container and cook for 15 minutes.
5. Present with your most loved plunging sauces.

Nutrition: Calories: 95, Carbs: 4 g, Fat: 7 g, Protein: 5 g

Griddle Fruit with Cream

 Prep Time 10 min   **Cook Time** 10 min   **Servings** 6

2 halved apricot
1 halved nectarine
2 halved peaches
1/4 cup blueberries
1/2 cup raspberries
2 tablespoons honey
1 orange, peel
2 cups cream
1/2 cup balsamic vinegar

1. Preheat the griddle to 400°F with a closed lid.
2. Griddle the peaches, nectarines, and apricots for 4 minutes on each side.
3. Place a pan over the stove and turn on medium heat. Add 2 tablespoons of honey, vinegar, and orange peel. Simmer until medium thick.
4. In the meantime, add honey and cream to a bowl. Whip until it reaches a soft form.
5. Place the fruits on a serving plate. Sprinkle with berries. Drizzle with balsamic reduction. Serve with cream and enjoy!

Nutrition: Calories: 230, Protein: 3 g, Carbs: 35 g, Fat: 3 g

Bacon Sweet Potato Pie

 Prep Time 20 min
 Cook Time 80 min
 Servings 4

1 pound 3 ounces sweet potatoes
1 1/4 cups plain yogurt
¾ cup packed, dark brown sugar
1/2 teaspoon cinnamon
1/4 teaspoon nutmeg
5 egg yolks
1/4 teaspoon salt
1 (up to 9 inches) deep dish, frozen pie shell
1 cup chopped pecans, toasted
4 strips of bacon, cooked and diced
1 tablespoon maple syrup
Optional: Whipped topping

1. First, shape the potatoes right into a steamer crate and sees into a good-sized pot of stew water. Ensure the water is not any nearer than creeps from the base of the bushel. When steamed for 20 mins, pound with a potato masher and let it in a safe spot.
2. While your flame broil is preheating, locate the sweet potatoes within the bowl of a stand blender and beat.
3. Include yogurt, dark-colored sugar, cinnamon, nutmeg, yolks, and salt, to flavor, and beat until very a whole lot joined. Take this hitter into the pie shell and see it onto a sheet dish. Sprinkle walnuts and bacon on pinnacle and bathe with maple syrup.
4. Heat for 45 to 60 mins or until the custard arrives at 165 to 180°F. Take out from the dish. Keep refrigerated in the wake of cooling.

Nutrition: Calories: 270, Carbs: 39 g, Fat: 12 g, Protein: 4 g

Apple Pie on the Griddle

 Prep Time 15 min
 Cook Time 40 min
 Servings 2

1/4 cup sugar
4 apples, sliced
1 tablespoon cornstarch
1 teaspoon cinnamon, ground
1 pie crust, refrigerated, soften according to the directions on the box
1/2 cup peach preserves

1. Preheat the griddle to 375°F with a closed lid.
2. In a bowl, combine the cinnamon, cornstarch, sugar, and apples. Set aside.
3. Place the pie crust in a pie pan. Spread the preserves and then place the apples. Fold the crust slightly.
4. Place a pan on the griddle (upside-down) so that you don't brill/bake the pie directly on the heat.
5. Cook 30 - 40 minutes. Once done, set aside to rest. Serve and enjoy

Nutrition: Calories: 160, Protein: 2 g, Carbs: 35 g, Fat: 1 g

Seasonal Fruit on the Griddle

 Prep Time 5 min
 Cook Time 5 min
 Servings 2

2 plums, peaches, apricots, etc. (choose seasonally)
3 tablespoons sugar, turbinate
1/4 cup honey
Gelato, as desired

1. Preheat the griddle to 450°F with a closed lid.
2. Slice each fruit in halves and remove the pits. Brush with honey. Sprinkle with some sugar.
3. Griddle on the grate until you see that there are griddle marks. Set aside.
4. Serve each with a scoop of gelato. Enjoy.

Nutrition: Calories: 120, Protein: 1 g, Carbs: 15 g, Fat: 3 g

Coconut Chocolate Simple Brownies

 Prep Time 10 min **Cook Time** 30 min **Servings** 4

4 eggs
1 cup cane sugar
¾ cup coconut oil
4 ounces chocolate, chopped
1/2 teaspoon sea salt
1/4 cup cocoa powder, unsweetened
1/2 cup flour
4 ounces chocolate chips
1 teaspoon vanilla

1. Preheat the griddle to 350°F with a closed lid.
2. Take a baking pan (9x9), grease it, and line a parchment paper.
3. In a bowl, combine the salt, cocoa powder, and flour. Stir and set aside.
4. In the microwave or double boiler, melt the coconut oil and chopped chocolate. Let it cool a bit.
5. Add the vanilla, eggs, and sugar. Whisk to combine.
6. Add into the flour, and add chocolate chips. Pour the mixture into a pan.
7. Place the pan on the grate. Bake for 20 minutes. If you want dryer brownies bake for 5-10 minutes more.
8. Let them cool before cutting.
9. Cut the brownies into squares and serve.

Nutrition: Calories: 135, Protein: 2 g, Carbs: 16 g, Fat: 3 g

2 pounds cake
3 cups whipped cream
1/4 cup melted butter
1 cup blueberries
1 cup raspberries
1 cup sliced strawberries

Griddle Layered Cake

 Prep Time 10 min **Cook Time** 14 min **Servings** 4

1. Preheat the griddle to high with a closed lid.
2. Slice the cake loaf (3/4 inch), about 10 per loaf. Brush both sides with butter.
3. Griddle for 7 minutes on each side. Set aside.
4. Once cooled completely, start layering your cake. Place cake, berries, then cream.
5. Sprinkle with berries and serve.

Nutrition: Calories: 160, Protein: 2 g, Carbs: 22 g, Fat: 6 g

Pineapple Sundae

 Prep Time 5 min **Cook Time** 5 min **Servings** 1

1/4 pineapple peeled and sliced
2 cups vanilla ice cream
1/4 cup whipped cream
1/4 cup sliced almonds

1. Preparing the Ingredients.
2. Let cool before chopping.
3. Griddle the pineapple until tender. Scoop ice cream into 2 serving dishes. Immediately before serving, top with pineapple, whipped cream, and sliced almonds.
4. You can also make an awesome dessert "salsa" by adding chopped strawberries and fresh mint.

Nutrition: Calories: 155, Fat: 15 g, Carbs: 4 g, Protein: 3 g

Strawberry Shortcake

Prep Time 5 min

Cook Time 5 min

Servings 3

4 eggs
1 cup cane sugar
¾ cup coconut oil
4 ounces chocolate, chopped
1/2 teaspoon sea salt
1/4 cup cocoa powder, unsweetened
1/2 cup flour
4 ounces chocolate chips
1 teaspoon vanilla

1. Preheat the griddle to 350°F with a closed lid.
2. Take a baking pan (9x9), grease it, and line a parchment paper.
3. In a bowl, combine the salt, cocoa powder, and flour. Stir and set aside.
4. In the microwave or double boiler, melt the coconut oil and chopped chocolate. Let it cool a bit.
5. Add the vanilla, eggs, and sugar. Whisk to combine.
6. Add into the flour, and add chocolate chips. Pour the mixture into a pan.
7. Place the pan on the grate. Bake for 20 minutes. If you want dryer brownies bake for 5-10 minutes more.
8. Let them cool before cutting.
9. Cut the brownies into squares and serve.

Nutrition: Calories: 135, Protein: 2 g, Carbs: 16 g, Fat: 3 g

---

Apple Cobbler

Prep Time 20 min

Cook Time 110 min

Servings 7

8 granny smith apples
1 cup sugar
1 stick of melted butter
1 teaspoon cinnamon
Pinch salt
1/2 cup brown sugar
2 eggs
2 teaspoons baking powder
2 cups plain flour
1 1/2 cup sugar

1. Peel and quarter apples, and place them into a bowl. Add in the cinnamon and one c. sugar. Stir well to coat and let it sit for one hour.
2. Preheat your griddle, with your lid closed, until it reaches 350°F.
3. In a large bowl, add the salt, baking powder, eggs, brown sugar, sugar, and flour. Mix until it forms crumbles.
4. Place apples into the rack. Add the crumble mixture on top and drizzle with melted butter.
5. Place on the griddle and cook for 50 minutes.

Nutrition: Calories: 152, Carbs: 26 g, Fat: 5 g, Protein: 1 g

---

Caramel Bananas

Prep Time 5 min

Cook Time 10 min

Servings 2

1/3 cup chopped pecans
1/2 cup sweetened condensed milk
4 slightly green bananas
1/2 cup brown sugar
2 tablespoons corn syrup
1/2 cup butter

1. Preheat your griddle, with the lid closed, until it reaches 350°F.
2. Place the milk, corn syrup, butter, and brown sugar into a heavy saucepan and bring to a boil for 5 minutes, simmer the mixture in low heat. Stir frequently.
3. Place the bananas with their peels on, on the griddle, and let them griddle for 5 minutes. Flip and cook for five minutes more. Peels will be dark and might split.
4. Place on a serving platter. Cut the ends off the bananas and split peel down the middle. Take the peel off the bananas and spoon caramel on top. Sprinkle with pecans.

Nutrition: Calories: 152, Carbs: 36 g, Fat: 1 g, Protein: 1 g

Chocolate Chip Cookies

 Prep Time 10 min **Cook Time** 17 min **Servings** 3

1 1/2 cup chopped walnuts
1 teaspoon vanilla
2 cups chocolate chips
1 teaspoon baking soda
2 1/2 cup plain flour
1/2 teaspoon salt
1 1/2 stick softened butter
2 eggs
1 cup brown sugar
1/2 cup sugar

1. Preheat your griddle, with your lid closed, until it reaches 350ºF.
2. Mix the baking soda, salt, and flour.
3. Cream the brown sugar, sugar, and butter. Mix in the vanilla and eggs until it comes together.
4. Slowly add in the flour while continuing to beat. Once all flour has been incorporated, add in the chocolate chips and walnuts. Using a spoon, fold into batter.
5. Place an aluminum foil onto the griddle. In an aluminum foil, drop a spoonful of dough and bake for 17 minutes.

Nutrition: Calories: 150, Carbs: 18 g, Fat: 5 g, Protein: 10 g

---

Strawberry Pizza

 Prep Time 5 min **Cook Time** 10 min **Servings** 7

1 (8-oz.) thin-crust pizza dough
1/4 cup caramel sauce
2 bananas, sliced and griddled
8 strawberries, halved and griddled
2 tablespoons chocolate sauce
2 tablespoons raspberry sauce
1/4 cup peanuts, chopped
toasted coconut or crumbled graham (optional)

1. Preparing the Ingredients.
2. Arrange pizza dough to fit on the griddle. Cook on both sides to the desired doneness.
3. Spread caramel sauce over the pizza. Layer with bananas and strawberries. Spry with chocolate and raspberry sauces. Top with peanuts. Cut pizza into 8 slices. Serve alone or with your favorite ice cream.
4. Sprinkling toasted coconut or crumbled graham crackers will add extra flavor and crunch!

Nutrition: Calories: 361, Fat: 3 g, Carbs: 14 g, Protein: 1.g

---

Cinnamon Sugar Pumpkin Seeds

 Prep Time 5 min **Cook Time** 25 min **Servings** 1

2 tablespoons sugar
1 tbsp Seeds from a pumpkin
1 teaspoon cinnamon
2 tablespoons melted butter

1. Preheat your griddle, with your lid closed, until it reaches 350ºF.
2. Clean the seeds and toss them in the melted butter. Add them to the sugar and cinnamon. Spread them out on a baking sheet, place them on the griddle, and cook for 25 minutes. Serve.

Nutrition: Calories: 127, Protein: 5 g, Carbs: 15 g, Fat: 21 g

Griddled Doughnut with Ice Cream

 Prep Time 5 min **Cook Time** 10 min **Servings** 4

4 apple cider doughnuts, sliced in half
2 pears, halved, cored, and sliced
4 cups vanilla ice cream
1/2 cup chocolate sauce whipped cream for serving

1. Preparing the Ingredients.
2. Arrange doughnut and pears halves on the griddle Pan.
3. Cook to desired doneness. Place the ice cream in a small baking pan and cover it with plastic wrap. Press flat, about 2 inches thick, then place the pan into the freezer. Cut ice cream into 8 discs the same size as the doughnuts. Place one doughnut half on each dish.
4. Layer with sliced pears and ice cream. Top with a second doughnut half. Repeat to make it a triple-decker. Spry with chocolate sauce and whipped cream before serving. The key to this recipe is to use the best seasonal fruit. Local orchards and farm stands will keep the variety of this recipe endless!

Nutrition: Calories: 105, Fat: 3 g, Carbs: 26 g, Protein: 2 g

1/2 cup sugar
1 tablespoon cinnamon
4 slices bread 1/4 cup margarine
15 baby marshmallows
1 (4.4-oz.) chocolate bar

1. Preparing the Ingredients.
2. In a bowl whisk the eggs. Mix in half and half, cinnamon, and almond extract. Soak bread in the egg batter for 5 minutes. Preheat the griddle pan on medium heat, for 3-4 minutes. Melt 2 tablespoons of butter onto the pan.
3. Cook the French toast to the desired doneness. Repeat until all are cooked. Serve with maple syrup and butter.

Griddled Cinnamon Toast

 Prep Time 5 min **Cook Time** 6 min **Servings** 4

1. Preparing the Ingredients.
2. Combine sugar and cinnamon in a bowl. Spread margarine over one side of each slice of bread. Sprinkle with cinnamon and sugar mixture. Arrange two slices of bread on the griddle, margarine side down. Cover each slice with marshmallows and half of the chocolate bar. Top with the remaining two slices of bread.
3. Cook on both sides, 3 minutes per side. Serve alone or with a tall glass of milk! As if this couldn't get any better, try a little peanut butter inside!

Nutrition: Calories: 231, Fat: 1 g, Carbs: 59 g, Protein: 0.6 g

Brioche French Toast

 Prep Time 7 min **Cook Time** 9 min **Servings** 5

10 eggs ¾ cup half and half
2 teaspoons cinnamon
1 teaspoon almond extract
1/4 cup maple syrup, to serve
1 loaf brioche bread, sliced
1 stick butter

Nutrition: Calories: 108, Fat: 9 g, Carbs: 4 g, Protein: 2 g

Griddled Banana Sundae

 Prep Time 15 min **Cook Time** 10 min **Servings** 2

Strawberry Sauce:
8 oz. strawberries
2 teaspoons sugar

Pineapple Sauce:
8 oz. pineapple rounds
1/4 cup light brown sugar
Sundae Basics

Strawberry sauce:

1. In a small saucepan, combine the griddled strawberries with sugar.
2. Griddle strawberries, pineapple, and banana halves to the desired doneness. Set aside.
3. Cook until sugar is dissolved and strawberries are blended.

Pineapple sauce:

4. In a separate saucepan, combine the griddled pineapples with light brown sugar. Cook until sugar is dissolved and pineapples are blended.
5. Assemble the sundae:
6. Line a dish with griddled bananas.
7. Top with 3 scoops of vanilla and/or chocolate ice cream and fruit sauces. Sprinkle with peanuts.
8. I love using this griddled fruit sauce to flavor my margaritas!

Nutrition: Calories: 90, Fat: 15 g, Carbs: 18 g, Protein: 2 g

Griddled Peaches and Berries with Ice Cream

 Prep Time 15 min **Cook Time** 65 min **Servings** 4

1/2 cup Simple Syrup
1 cup Water
1/2 cup sugar
1 cinnamon stick orange liqueur
2 peaches, halved and pitted
6 strawberries, halved
Vanilla ice cream
1/2 cup fresh blueberries mint
4 slice flatbread

Simple syrup:

1. Bring water, sugar, and cinnamon stick to a boil. Add orange liqueur.
2. Combine peaches and strawberries in a bowl with simple syrup. Soak for 1 hour at room temperature.
3. Set the griddle on high heat. Cook strawberries and peaches until tender. Top ice cream with griddled fruit. Garnish with blueberries and fresh mint immediately before serving.
4. I love combining flatbread, chocolate hazelnut spread, and griddled fruit for an amazing dessert pizza!

Nutrition: Calories: 230, Fat: 24 g, Carbs: 8 g, Protein: 6 g

2 tablespoons butter
3 tablespoons brown sugar
3 apples, cored and sliced
2 sheets of puff pastry
1 egg yolk
1 tablespoon milk
1/2 teaspoons nutmeg
1 teaspoon cinnamon

Griddled Apple Pie

 Prep Time 15 min **Cook Time** 35 min **Servings** 2

1. Melt butter and brown sugar in a saucepot. Add apples. Cook, tossing occasionally, for 5 minutes or until tender. Set aside to cool.

2. Arrange 1 sheet of puff pastry onto the unheated griddle. In a bowl, mix egg yolk and milk. Use to brush edges of puff pastry.

3. Toss apples with nutmeg and cinnamon. Arrange apple slices on top of the puff pastry. Leave one inch of pastry untouched on all sides.

4. Preheat the oven to 400°F. Top apples with the second sheet of puff pastry. Seal on all sides.

5. Cook on medium-low heat for about 10 minutes.

6. Brush the top with egg and milk mixture. Bake in the oven for 15 minutes or until golden. Allow the pie to cool.

7. Cut and serve with vanilla ice cream and caramel sauce. If they are in season, sprinkle some fresh berries on top of the apples before placing the top puff pastry

Nutrition: Calories: 360, Fat: 33 g, Carbs: 13 g, Protein: 6 g

Pound Cake and Fruit

 Prep Time 5 min **Cook Time** 10 min **Servings** 6

6 slices of pound cake
3 peaches, sliced and pitted
3 bananas, peeled and sliced
24 large strawberries
1/2 cup simple syrup
1/4 cup raspberry sauce
1 cup whipped cream
6 mint leaves, for garnish

1. Arrange the pound cake, peaches, bananas, and strawberries on the griddle Pan.

2. Cook on both sides to the desired doneness. Toss the fruit with simple syrup. Set aside. Plate the pound cake with griddled fruit. Top with raspberry sauce and whipped cream. Garnish with mint leaves immediately before serving.

3. Another delicious variation in this recipe is to slice a corn muffin in half and griddle it. The fruit and cream complement the corn's sweetness.

Nutrition: Calories: 173, Fat: 4 g, Carbs: 37 g, Protein: 3 g

Griddled Fruit Skewers

 Prep Time 10 min

 Cook Time 10 min

 Servings 5

1. Skewer the cut fruit.
2. Cook to desired doneness.

Dipping sauce:

3. In a saucepot, bring the heavy cream to a boil. Add the chocolate chips and remove them from the heat. Mix until creamy, then add vanilla. Serve griddled fruit with chocolate dipping sauce.
4. Feel free to choose any chocolate you like. Dark and white work well with this recipe.

8 strawberries, large
2 peaches, sliced thick
1 pear, sliced thick
1 cup pineapple, cubed
1 banana, sliced thick

Chocolate Dipping Sauce:
1 cup heavy cream
1 cup semi-sweet chocolate chips
1/2 teaspoons vanilla extract

Nutrition: Calories: 183, Fat: 8 g, Carbs: 31 g, Protein: 3 g

Griddled Apple Bowl

 Prep Time 15 min

 Cook Time 3 min

 Servings 4

Simple syrup:

1. In a saucepan, bring the sugar, water, and cinnamon stick to a boil. Set aside.
2. Cut the apples in half and core with a melon baller. Add to the simple syrup. Arrange apples on the griddle Pan, cut side down.
3. Cook for 3 minutes. Turn over and continue cooking until tender. Baste with simple syrup. Top the apples with ice cream, caramel sauce, and chopped pecans immediately before serving. These apples can also be made in advance.
4. Cool in the refrigerator. When you are ready to serve, warm up in the microwave.

Simple Syrup:
1 cup sugar
1 cup water
1 cinnamon stick
2 apples, large
2 cups vanilla ice cream
1/2 cup caramel sauce
1/2 cup pecans, chopped

Nutrition: Calories: 183, Fat: 8 g, Carbs: 31 g, Protein: 3 g

Honey Griddled Peaches

 Prep Time 10 min   **Cook Time** 10 min   **Servings** 3

Fresh peaches, as desired
Fresh honey, as desired
Cinnamon to taste
Coconut oil, as needed
Plain yogurt or ice cream for topping

Nutrition: Calories: 132, Carbs: 32 g, Fat: 0 g, Protein: 13 g

1. Slice the peaches lengthwise from top to bottom and remove the pits. Drizzle honey on the cut side of the peach and sprinkle with cinnamon.
2. Bring the griddle to medium-low heat. Oil the Griddle and allow it to heat until the oil is shimmering but not smoking.
3. Set the peaches sliced side up and cook them for a couple of minutes cut side down, then flip and brush with coconut oil honey, and cinnamon
4. Griddle for several minutes until the skin starts to brown and pull back. Serve with vanilla ice cream while still warm.

Banana Cinnamon Coconut Fritters

 Prep Time 5 min   **Cook Time** 4 min   **Servings** 2

2 bananas, mashed
1/3 cup flour
1/2 teaspoons cinnamon
2 eggs
1/2 cup shredded coconut

1. Combine all fixings except oil in a bowl.
2. Preheat the griddle pan for 4 minutes on medium heat.
3. Coat the pan with canola oil.
4. Drop heaping tablespoons of fritter batter onto the pan.
5. Serve.

Nutrition: Calories: 115, Carbs: 11 g, Fat: 7 g, Protein: 2 g

Rosemary Watermelon Steaks

 Prep Time 10 min   **Cook Time** 10 min **Servings** 1

1. Heat a griddle for medium heat. Cut the watermelon into 2-inch-thick slices, with the rind intact, and then into halves or quarters, if you like.
2. Place the oil and rosemary in a small bowl, sprinkle with salt and pepper, and stir. Brush or rub this batter all over the watermelon slices.
3. Place the watermelon on the griddle directly. Cook turning once until the flesh has dried out a bit, 4 to 5 minutes per side. Transfer it to your platter and serve with lemon wedges.

1 small watermelon, removed seeds
1/4 cup good-quality olive oil
1 tablespoon minced fresh rosemary
Salt and pepper, as needed
Lemon wedges for serving

Nutrition: Calories: 101, Carbs: 11 g, Fat: 0 g, Protein: 2 g

Griddled Pineapple Disk with Vanilla Bean Ice Cream

 Prep Time 5 min **Cook Time** 10 min **Servings** 7

1 whole pineapple, sliced into 6 equal slices
6 scoops of vanilla bean ice cream
6 spoonsful of whipped cream
1/4 cup almond slivers, toasted
1/4 cup sweetened shredded coconut, toasted
1/2 cup caramel sauce
Mint (to garnish)

1. Bring the griddle to medium-low heat. Oil your griddle and allow it to heat until the oil is shimmering but not smoking. Cook pineapple until a nice char forms, about 2 minutes per side.
2. Remove pineapple from the griddle, and top each slice with a scoop of ice cream, a dollop of whipped cream, almonds, and coconut. Drizzle each with caramel sauce, garnish with mint, and serve.

Nutrition: Calories: 140, Carbs: 19 g, Fat: 6 g, Protein: 2 g

Buttered Popcorn

 Prep Time 5 min **Cook Time** 4 min **Servings** 1

3 tablespoons peanut oil
1/2 cup popcorn kernels
3 tablespoons butter
Salt, to taste

1. Prepare your griddle for two-zone cooking. Set the griddle to medium-high heat and add the peanut oil. While it is heating, place 5 popcorn kernels in the oil.
2. When 2 or 3 pop, add the butter to the oil and pour in the remaining kernels. Cover immediately with a tall pan or spaghetti pot.
3. When the popcorn starts popping, you will need to stir it in the oil to get all the kernels to pop and prevent the popped corn from burning.
4. Using insulated gloves, potholders, or thick kitchen towels, agitate the popcorn by moving the pan or pot from side to side on the griddle without lifting.
5. Cook within 4 minutes, or until the popping slows down to once every few seconds. When all the corn is popped, slide the pot or pan and popcorn to the cool side of the griddle and remove the lid.
6. Use two spatulas to scoop up the hot popcorn and transfer it to a bowl. Serve with salt and additional seasonings as desired.

Nutrition: Calories: 170, Carbs: 13 g, Fat: 12 g, Protein: 2 g

Bourbon Cocktail with Griddle Blood Orange

1. Preheat the griddle to medium-high heat and brush with olive oil. Cut 3 of the oranges in half and cook, cut side down, over high heat until charred.
2. Halve the remaining orange, cut into thick slices, and cook until charred on both sides; set aside. Squeeze the orange halves to get 1 cup of juice.
3. Add the juice, bourbon, and sugar to a cocktail shaker. Add ice to fill the shaker almost to the rim. Shake well for about 60 seconds to ensure the sugar dissolves and the drink is well chilled.
4. Strain into a sugar-rimmed coupe or martini glasses and garnish each with a charred orange slice.

 Prep Time 5 min **Cook Time** 10 min **Servings** 2

3 tablespoons peanut oil
1/2 cup popcorn kernels
3 tablespoons butter
Salt, to taste

Nutrition: Calories: 120, Carbs: 30 g, Fat: 0 g, Protein: 5 g

No Bake Energy Bites

 Prep Time 5 min  **Cook Time** 0 min **Servings** 1

1 cup (dry) oatmeal
1/2 cup chocolate chips
1/2 cup peanut butter
1/2 cup ground flaxseed
1/3 cup honey
1 tsp. vanilla

1. Mix all ingredients and roll into balls.
2. Store in the fridge or freezer for a little treat instead of a candy bar!

Nutrition: Calories: 93, Fat: 1 g, Carbs: 22 g, Protein: 2 g

Avocado Quesadillas

 Prep Time 15 min **Cook Time** 10 min **Servings** 6

1 tablespoon canola oil
16 corn tortillas
2 cups Mexican cheese, shredded
1 cup Pico de Gallo
1 large ripe avocado, peeled and thinly sliced
3 tablespoons cilantro, minced and fresh

1. Oil a griddle and cook it over medium heat. To moisten the tortillas, lightly sprinkle them with water.
2. On a griddle, place eight tortillas and top with cheese. Top with avocado, Pico de Gallo, and cilantro when the cheese has somewhat melted. Add the remaining tortillas on top.
3. Cook for 3-5 minutes on each side or till cheese is melted and lightly browned. Serve with more Pico de Gallo on the side.

Nutrition: Calories: 611, Fat: 37 g, Carbs: 54 g, Protein: 20 g

Golden Zucchini Pancakes

 Prep Time 5 min **Cook Time** 15 min **Servings** 5

3 cups zucchini, shredded
2 large eggs
2 minced garlic cloves
3/4 teaspoons salt
1/2 teaspoons pepper
1/4 teaspoon dried oregano
1/2 cup all-purpose flour
1/2 cup sweet onion, finely chopped
1 tablespoon butter
Marinara sauce, warmed

1. Drain zucchini in a colander, pressing hard to remove excess water.
2. In a large mixing bowl, whisk together the eggs, salt, garlic, pepper, and oregano until well combined. Stir in the flour until it is just moistened. Combine zucchini and onion in a mixing bowl.
3. Using butter, lightly coat a griddle and cook over medium heat. Drop 1/4 cupful of zucchini mixture over griddle; flatten to 1/2-inch thickness. Cook for 4-6 minutes on each side, or until golden brown.
4. Serve with marinara sauce on the side, if desired.

Nutrition: Calories: 145, Fat: 6 g, Carbs: 18 g, Protein: 6 g

Carrot Cake Pancakes

 Prep Time 5 min   **Cook Time** 10 min   **Servings** 4

2 cups pancake mix
1 teaspoon ground cinnamon
1/4 teaspoons ground nutmeg
1/8 teaspoons ground cloves
2 large eggs
1 cup whole milk
1 cup carrots, finely shredded

For topping:
1/2 cup maple syrup
1/8 teaspoons ground cinnamon
2/3 cup whipped cream
1 tablespoon whole milk
1/2 cup walnuts or pecans, chopped
Carrots, finely shredded

1. Mix the cinnamon, pancake mix, nutmeg, and cloves in a large mixing bowl. In a small bowl, whisk together the eggs and milk; whisk just until the dry ingredients are moistened. Toss in the carrots.
2. Pour 1/4 cupful of batter onto a hot oiled griddle. When bubbles appear on top of the pancakes, flip them and cook until the other side is golden brown.
3. To make the syrup, mix the maple syrup and cinnamon in a small saucepan. Bring to a boil. Reduce heat to low and cook for 2 minutes. Mix milk and cream cheese in a small mixing bowl. Serve pancakes, cheese mixture, and half of the syrup; top with nuts and shredded carrots, if preferred. Save the remaining syrup by covering it and refrigerating it.

Nutrition: Calories: 388, Fat: 16 g, Carbs: 52 g, Protein: 10 g

Griddled Pear Crisp

 Prep Time 5 min   **Cook Time** 20 min   **Servings** 4

2 pears, cored
Crisp Topping:
1/4 cup brown sugar
1/4 cup flour
3 tablespoons butter
2 tablespoons walnuts
1/2 teaspoons cinnamon
2 cups vanilla ice cream
4 tablespoons caramel sauce
1/4 cup crisp topping

1. Griddle pears until tender. About 5 minutes per side. Make crisp topping: combine brown sugar, flour, butter, walnuts, and cinnamon in a bowl.
2. Bake in the oven for 15 minutes at 400°F. Place half a pear into each serving bowl. Immediately before serving, top with 1/2 cup vanilla ice cream, 2 tablespoons crisp topping, and 1 tablespoon caramel sauce.
3. Feel free to substitute any ripe fruit in seasons, such as local apples or peaches.

Nutrition: Calories: 190, Fat: 17 g, Carbs: 5 g, Protein: 5 g

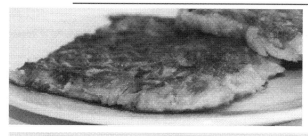

Griddled Pear Crisp

 Prep Time 5 min   **Cook Time** 20 min   **Servings** 4

2 lbs. potatoes, peeled
2 large eggs, lightly beaten
1 tablespoon grated onion
2 tablespoons all-purpose flour
1 teaspoon salt
1/2 teaspoons baking powder
Vegetable oil, for frying

1. Potatoes should be finely grated. Any liquid should be drained. Combine the eggs, flour, onion, salt, and baking powder in a mixing bowl.
2. Add 1/8 inch of oil to a frying pan and heat over moderate flame.
3. Drop heaping tablespoonsful of batter into the hot oil.
4. Make patties out of the mixture. Fry, turning once, until golden brown. Serve immediately.

Nutrition: Calories: 257, Fat: 8 g, Carbs: 41 g, Protein: 6 g

Conclusion

Griddles can be used in a variety of ways. By now, I'm sure you've realized that with a flat-top griddle, you can cook almost any kind of meat, vegetable, or fish. It's the ideal companion for every party or social event you may have in the summer months, and with little care also all year round. It's versatile, sturdy, and easy to clean, which makes it a perfect choice for every home.

To get the best performance out of your griddle, we recommend you follow these tips:

Before using any cooking device, please read the instruction booklet carefully. It will give you very useful information on how to use it safely and effectively. If you have any doubts about the correct use of each machine before operating one, you must make sure that it is in perfect mechanical shape.

I am sure you have found lots of recipes that have made you fall in love with your griddle. All you have to do is keep using and creating even more recipes and variations on the ones you have found here. Little by little, mate with your griddle and let it become part of your daily routine. It will for sure become a truly beloved piece of equipment for all you devoted griddle freaks and foodies.

I have tried as best as possible to show you how versatile a griddle can be, hoping that it will inspire you to be creative and try new dishes that are also easily adaptable to any season.

Have fun, enjoy your food and make the life of those around you a little better with the delicious taste of your favorite meals using your fantastic Griddle!

Made in the USA
Monee, IL
10 October 2022

15541420R00072